EUROPE IN 22 DAYS

A STEP-BY-STEP GUIDE AND TRAVEL ITINERARY

BY RICK STEVES

EDITED BY GENE OPENSHAW

Copyright © 1985, 1987 by Rick Steves
Cover copyright © 1987 by John Muir Publications
All Rights Reserved

Revised edition

Library of Congress Catalog No. 86-043097

Published by John Muir Publications
Santa Fe, New Mexico
Printed in U.S.A.

Maps   David C. Hoerline
Cover   Jennifer Dewey
Design/Production   Mary Shapiro
Typography   Copygraphics, Inc.
Editorial   Gene Openshaw

ISBN 0-912528-62-1

CONTENTS

Europe

HOW TO USE THIS BOOK

This book is the tour guide in your pocket. It lets you be the boss by giving you the best basic 22 days in Europe and a suggested way to use each of those days most efficiently. It is for do-it-yourselfers—with or without a tour.

Europe in 22 Days originated (and is still used) as the tour handbook for those who join me on my "Back Door Europe" Tours. Since most large organized tours work to keep their masses ignorant while visiting many of the same places we'll cover, this book is a self-defense manual for anyone who wants to maintain independence and flexibility while taking a typical big bus tour.

Realistically, most travelers are interested in the predictable biggies—Rhine castles, Sistine Chapel, Eiffel Tower and beerhalls. This tour covers those while mixing in a good dose of "back door intimacy"—Italian hilltowns, forgotten Riviera ports and traffic-free Swiss Alp villages.

While the trip is designed as a car tour (3,000 miles), it also makes a great three-week train trip. Each day's journey is adapted for train travel with explanations, options and appropriate train schedules included.

A three-week car rental (split two ways) or a three-week first class Eurailpass costs $350 at this writing. It costs $500 to $800 to fly roundtrip to Amsterdam. For room and board figure $30 a day for 22 days, totaling $660. This is a feasible budget if you know the tricks—see *Europe Through the Back Door.* Add $200 or $300 fun money and you've got yourself a great European adventure for under $2,000. Do it!

Of course, connect-the-dots travel isn't perfect, just as color-by-numbers ain't good art. But this book is your friendly Frenchman, your German in a jam, your handbook. It's your well-thought-out and tested itinerary. . . I've done it—and refined it—twenty times on my own and with groups. Use it, take advantage of it, but don't let it rule you. Try to travel outside of peak season, July and August, so finding hotels won't be a problem; wear a moneybelt; use local tourist information centers; and work to fit in, travel as a temporary local person.

Read this book from cover to cover and then use it as a rack to hang more ideas on as your trip evolves. As you study and travel and plan and talk to people you'll fill it with notes. It's your tool. The book is completely modular and is adaptable to any European trip. You'll find 22 units—or days—each built with the same sections:

1. **Introductory overview** for the day.
2. **Suggested Schedule** for the day.
3. **Transportation** plan for drivers, plus an adapted plan with schedules for train travelers.
4. List of **Sightseeing Highlights** (rated: ▲▲▲Don't miss; ▲▲Try hard to see; ▲Worthwhile if you can make it); **Helpful Hints** on orientation, shopping, transportation, day-to-day chores, timing.
5. An easy-to-read **map** locating all recommended places.
6. **Food and Lodging:** How and where to find the best budget places, including addresses, phone numbers, and my favorites.
7. **Optional itinerary** for those with more or less than the suggested time, or with particular interests. This itinerary is rubbery!

For each country there is also a **culture review** and **practical phrase list**. The back of the book includes post-trip options, several suggested regional 22-day trips, a climate chart and list of local festivals for 1987, a complete youth hostel directory for the route and more.

Efficient Travelers Think Ahead
This itinerary assumes you are a well-organized traveler who lays departure groundwork upon arrival, reads a day ahead in the itinerary book, keeps a list of all the things that should be taken care of, and avoids problems whenever possible before they happen.

When to Go, Timing
The best months to travel are May, June, September or October. Peak season (July and August) is most difficult. During this very crowded time it's best to arrive early in the day and call hotels in advance (call from one hotel to the next; your receptionist can help you). Things like banking, laundry stops, good mail days and picnics should be anticipated and planned for. If you expect to travel smart, you will. If you insist on being confused, your trip will be a mess.

Prices
For simplicity I've priced things throughout this book in dollars. These prices, as well as the hours, telephone numbers and so on, are accurate as of August 1986. Since admission to sights and museums is generally about a dollar, I've left most of them out. Things are always changing and I have tossed timidity out the window knowing you'll understand that this book, like

any guidebook, starts growing old even before it's printed. Please don't expect Europe to have stood entirely still since this book was written, and do what you can to call ahead or double-check hours and times when you arrive.

Border Crossings
Passing from one country to another in Europe is generally extremely easy. Sometimes you won't even realize it's happened. When you do change countries, however, you change money, postage stamps, and much more. Plan ahead for these changes. (Coins and stamps are worthless outside of their home countries).

Language and Culture
You will be dealing with an intensely diverse language and customs situation; work to adapt. The USA is huge but it's bound by common language. The cultural stew of Europe is wonderfully complex. We just assume Germany is "Germany"; but Germany is "Tedesco" to the Italians, "Allemagne" to the French, and "Deutschland" to the people who live there. While we think shower curtains are logical, many countries just cover the toilet paper and let the rest of the room shower with you. Europeans give their "ones" an upswing and cross their "sevens." If you don't adapt, your "seven" will be mistaken for a sloppy "one" and you'll miss your train.

Scheduling
Your overall itinerary strategy is a fun challenge. Read through this book and note the problem days when most museums are closed (i.e. Paris—Tuesday; Florence and Amsterdam—Monday). Remember, many museums and sights, especially large ones and those in Italy, stop admitting people 30 minutes before closing time. Sundays have the same pros and cons as they do for travelers in the USA. (Traffic in cities is light. Sightseeing attractions are generally open, but shops, banks, etc. are closed. Rowdy evenings are rare on Sundays.) Saturdays in Europe are virtually weekdays with earlier closing hours. It's good to mix intense and relaxed periods. Every trip needs at least a few slack days. I've built the itinerary with every stop but one (Rhine) for two nights in a row. This makes the speed of the tour much more manageable.

Speed
This itinerary is fast. If all goes well it can be done with minimal hecticity. But all won't go well. A few slack days come in very handy. Eurailers should streamline with overnight train rides.

I've listed many more sights than any mortal tourist could possibly see in 22 days. They are rated so you can carefully make the difficult choices to shape your most comfortable, smooth and rewarding trip.

Keeping Up with the News (If You Must)

To keep in touch with world and American news while traveling in Europe, I use the International Herald Tribune which comes out almost daily via satellite from many places in Europe. Every Tuesday the European editions of Time and Newsweek hit the stands. They are full of articles of particular interest to European travelers.

Remember, news in English will only be sold where there's enough demand—in big cities and tourist centers. If you are concerned about how some event might affect your safety as an American traveling abroad, call the U.S. consulate or embassy in the nearest big city for advice.

Terrorism

Terrorism has no business affecting your travel plans. I spent ("survived") the summer of '86 in southern Europe. The general feeling there among locals and travelers was 1) Reagan decided to keep America home this year to boost our economy, and 2) our media loves a crisis—and if there isn't one handy they'll create it. I felt no unusual anti-American sentiment and I traveled knowing that, regardless of what Ronald Reagan, Dan Rather and my grandma say, you're safer (and happier) traveling in Europe.

Recommended Guidebooks

This small book is your itinerary handbook. To really enjoy and appreciate these busy three weeks, you'll also need some directory-type guidebook information. I know it hurts to spend $30 or $40 on extra guidebooks, but when you consider the improvements they will make in your $2,000 vacation—not to mention the money they'll save you—not buying them would be perfectly "penny-wise and pound-foolish." Here is my recommended guidebook strategy.

General low-budget directory-type guidebook—You need one. *Let's Go: Europe* is the best. If its youthful approach is not yours, then Arthur Frommer's individual country guidebooks are next best (for Germany, France and Italy). Frommer's *Europe on $25 a Day* is helpful only for the big cities. For this trip, you can just rip out the chapters on Venice, Rome, Florence and Paris. If you like the *Let's Go* style, the individual books in that series (Italy and France) are the best anywhere.

Cultural and sightseeing guides—The tall green Michelin guides (Germany, Austria, Italy, Switzerland, Paris) have nothing about room and board but everything else you'll ever need to know about the sights, customs and culture. I found the new little blue American Express Guides to Venice, Florence, Rome and Paris even handier than the Michelin, but expensive.

Phrase books—Unless you speak German, Italian and French, you'd better cover your linguistic bases with a phrase book. Berlitz puts out great pocket guides to each of those languages as well as a little book with 14 European languages covered more briefly (but adequately for me). Berlitz also has a pocket-sized 14-language menu phrase book ideal for those galloping gluttons who plan to eat their way through Europe. Frommer's *Fast n' Easy Phrase Book* covering Europe's four major languages (German, Italian, French and Spanish) is new and ideal for our itinerary.

Rick Steves' books—Finally, I've written this book assuming you've read or will read the latest editions of my books *Europe Through the Back Door* and *Europe 101*.

To keep this book small and pocket-sized, I have resisted the temptation to repeat the most applicable and important information already included in my other books; there is no overlap.

Europe Through the Back Door gives you the basic skills, the foundation which makes this demanding 22-day plan possible. Chapters on: minimizing jet lag, packing light, driving or train travel, finding budget beds without reservations, changing money, theft and the tourist, tourism and terrorism, hurdling the language barrier, health, travel photography, ugly-Americanism, laundry, and itinerary strategies and techniques that are so important. The book also includes special articles on 32 "Back Doors," eight of which are included in this tour (Hilltowns, Civita, Cinqueterre, Romantic Road, Castle Day, Swiss Alps, Alsace and Versailles).

Europe 101 gives you the story of Europe's people, history and art. Your bookstore should have these two books (available through John Muir Publications), or you can order directly using the order form in the back of this book.

Books I would buy for this trip: (1) *Let's Go: Europe* (rip out appropriate chapters) $10.95, (2) *Europe on $25 a Day* (take only applicable chapters) $10.95, (3) Frommer's *Fast n' Easy Phrase Book*, $6.95, (4) Michelin's Green Guide for Italy, $9.95. That comes to $38, or $19 each for two people.

I'd read *Europe Through the Back Door* and *Europe 101* at home before departing. Of all the books mentioned, only the Michelin guides are available in Europe; better yet, they are available in English and are cheaper there than in the USA.

My goal is to free you, not chain you. Please defend your spontaneity like you would your mother, and use this book to avoid time- and money-wasting mistakes, to get more intimate with Europe by traveling as a temporary local person, and as a point of departure from which to shape your best possible travel experience.

Anyone who has read this far has what it takes intellectually to do this tour independently. Be confident, enjoy the hills and the valleys. Judging from all the positive feedback and happy postcards we get from travelers who used earlier editions of *Europe in 22 Days*, it's safe to assume you're on your way to a great European vacation—independent, inexpensive and with the finesse of an experienced traveler. Europe, here you come!

BACK DOOR TRAVEL PHILOSOPHY
AS TAUGHT IN EUROPE THROUGH THE BACK DOOR

TRAVEL IS INTENSIFIED LIVING—maximum thrills per minute and one of the last great sources of legal adventure. In many ways, the less you spend the more you get.

Experiencing the real thing requires candid informality—going "Through the Back Door."

Affording travel is a matter of priorities. Many people who "can't afford a trip" could sell their car and travel for two years.

You can travel anywhere in the world for $25 a day plus transportation costs. Money has little to do with enjoying your trip. In fact, in many ways, the less you spend the more you get—spending more money only builds a thicker wall between you and what you came to see.

A tight budget forces you to travel "close to the ground," meeting and communicating with the people, not relying on service with a purchased smile. Never sacrifice sleep, nutrition, safety or cleanliness in the name of budget. Simply enjoy the local-style alternatives to expensive hotels and restaurants.

Extroverts have more fun. If your trip is low on magic moments, kick yourself and start making things happen. Dignity and good travel don't mix. Leave your beeper at home and let your hair down.

If you don't enjoy a place it's often because you don't know enough about it. Seek out the truth. Recognize tourist traps.

A culture is legitimized by its existence. Give a people the benefit of your open mind. Think of things as different but not better or worse.

Of course, travel, like the world, is a series of hills and valleys. Be fanatically positive and militantly optimistic.

Travel is addicting. It can make you a happier American, as well as a citizen of the world. Our Earth is home to five billion equally important people. That's wonderfully humbling.

Globetrotting destroys ethnocentricity and encourages the understanding and appreciation of various cultures. Travel changes people. Many travelers toss aside their "hometown blinders," assimiliating the best points of different cultures into their own character.

The world is a cultural garden. We're working on the ultimate salad. Won't you join us?

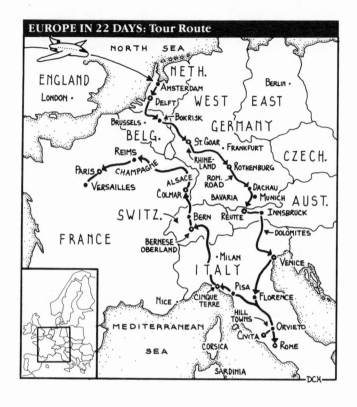

EUROPE IN 22 DAYS: Tour Route

ITINERARY

DAY 1 Depart.

DAY 2 Arrive at Amsterdam's Schipol Airport (usually the next day). Pick up car or activate Eurailpass. Drive to Delft or Haarlem, small towns outside of Amsterdam, check into hotel.

DAY 3 (All breakfasts are served in hotel at about 7:30 or 8:00.) Drive to Amsterdam. Orientation tour, visit Anne Frank's house, 3 hours to tour Van Gogh and Rijksmuseum, picnic lunch in park, 1 hour canal tour, 1 hour free to explore or shop. Return to home town for Indonesian feast, "Rice Table." Evening free in very typical Dutch town.

DAY 4 Drive to Belgian open-air folk museum at Bokrijk, largest and best in Low Countries. With local guided folk life tour. Picnic lunch. Drive into Germany. Check into a gasthaus on the Rhine. Dinner below a floodlit castle.

DAY 5 Tour largest castle on Rhine, Rheinfels. Cruise from St. Goar to Bacharach past most famous castles on Rhine. Picnic in park at Bacharach with free time in town. Drive via autobahn to Rothenburg. Dinner in gasthaus within medieval town walls.

DAY 6 Pre-breakfast walk around city wall. Morning introductory tour. Rest of day free for sightseeing or shopping. Best shopping town in Germany. Evening is best spent in a winestube or beerhall.

DAY 7 Morning, explore the Romantic Road, Germany's medieval heartland. Tour the concentration camp at Dachau. Picnic (possibly at Munich's Olympic Stadium) before driving farther south. Dinner and evening in Tyrolian town of Reutte.

DAY 8 "Castle Day" today. Beat the crowds to "Mad King" Ludwig's magnificent Neuschwanstein Castle. Visit the best example of Bavarian Baroque-Rococo style church architecture, the Wies Church. Time to explore busy Oberammergau before returning to your Austrian homebase to climb to the ruined castles of Ehrenburg and ride an alpine luge. Evening free to find some Tyrolian fun.

DAY 9 Morning free in Innsbruck's historic center with time to enjoy its great Tyrolian folk museum. Picnic at the Olympic ski jump, then a wondrous Alpine drive into sunny Italy. Evening cruise down Venice's Grand Canal, orientation tour and check into your very central hotel. After a typical Venetian dinner enjoy gelato, cappuccino, and the magical atmosphere of St. Mark's at night!

DAY 10 Morning tour of highlights of Venice—Doge's Palace, St. Mark's, the belltower. Rest of day free for shopping or art. Evening, famous "Back Door Venetian Pub Crawl Dinner."

DAY 11 Leave very early for three hour drive to Florence. All day in Europe's art capital with tour covering David, the Duomo and other highlights. Free time for shopping or more museums. Evening drive into Rome.

DAY 12 Walk through classical Rome—Colosseum, Forum, Capitol Hill. Lunch and siesta at hotel or convent. Afternoon visit St. Peter's, Europe's greatest basilica. Time to climb the 300-foot high dome for great city view. Evening walk through Trastevere, over the Tiber River to the colorful Campo dei Fiori for dinner, and on to Piazza Navona for Tartufo ice cream, people-watching and the floodlit Trevi Fountain.

DAY 13 Morning free to shop or sightsee or snooze. Afternoon to enjoy the Vatican Museum and Michaelangelo's Sistine Chapel. Evening drive north to Bagnoregio near Orvieto to the hilltown craziness of Angelino's place, a great feast, homemade wine, a possible "in-house disco" and a trip into "La Cantina"—memorable, to say the least.

DAY 14 All day to explore hilltowns. Morning visit to cute little Civita. Lunch in its only piazza. Afternoon to explore an Etruscan tomb (500 B.C.) and the famous hilltown of Orvieto. Evening back at Angelino's for dinner and more Italian fun.

DAY 15 Drive north to Cinqueterre. Lunch and time to climb Pisa's tipsy tower. Afternoon leave car in La Spezia and take train into the Italian Riviera. Vernazza is our headquarters village for this vacation from our vacation. Fresh seafood and local wine at Sr. Sorriso's Pension—the only place to stay in this traffic-free town. Evening is yours—be careful, there's lots of romance on the breakwater.

DAY 16 All day free for hiking, exploring villages, swimming, relaxing on the beach. Fun in the sun. You'll fall in love with the Italian Riviera. Dinner at Sorriso's. Evening free.

DAY 17 Leave very early. Drive along Riviera to Genoa, then north past Milan into Switzerland. After a stop in Italian Switzerland, Ticino, you climb over Susten Pass and into the heart of the Swiss Alps, the Bernese Oberland. After a stop in Interlaken, you'll ride the gondola to the stop just before heaven, Gimmelwald. This traffic-free alpine fairytale village has only one chalet-hotel, Hotel Mittaghorn, and that's where you'll stay. Walter will have a hearty dinner waiting.

DAY 18 Today is hike day. You'll spend the day memorably above the clouds in the region of the Jungfrau and the Eiger. Dinner with fondue at Walter's. Evening massage, coffee-schnapps and Swiss chocolate.

DAY 19 Free day. Optional lift up to the 10,000-foot Schilthorn for breakfast and hike down. Or sit in a meadow and be Heidi. Or shop and explore one of the villages of Lauterbrunnen Valley. Early dinner at Walter's (he's every Back Door tour's favorite cook) before driving out of Switzerland and into France. Evening in Colmar, Alsace where you'll check into the Hotel Le Rapp.

DAY 20 All day to explore historic Colmar and the Wine Road (Route du Vin) of the Alsace region. Lovely villages, wine tasting tours, and some powerful art. Evening is free in Colmar.

DAY 21 Long drive to Paris with mid-day stop for a picnic in Reims. Tour Reims' magnificent cathedral with a lesson in Gothic architecture. This is Champagne country and you can also tour a Champagne cave—free tasting, of course. Evening floodlit orientation tour of Paris with a chance to see all of the most famous landmarks.

DAY 22 Morning tour of Latin Quarter, Notre Dame, Ile de la Cite, Louvre Museum and historic center of Paris. Afternoon free for more sights or shopping. Evening trip up to Montmartre for a grand view, people-watching, crepes, visit to Sacre Coeur church and free time to enjoy the Bohemian artists' quarter.

Next day, tour Versailles, Europe's greatest palace.
Your plane will fly you home from Amsterdam ($35 train ride, 5 hours from Paris) on the day of your choice.

Basic Options
If you have a few extra days (or don't mind skipping Amsterdam) you can start this tour in London. After three nights and two days there and possible day trips to Bath and/or Cambridge, catch the

$30, 8- to 10-hour trip to Belgium or Holland. Boats go daily overnight from England to the Hoek van Holland (near Delft) or Oostende (near the great town of Brugge). From Paris you're an easy 8-hour trip to London and your return flight.

To add Greece, consider starting in London, doing this 22-day tour with Paris first and Switzerland before Italy, then catching the boat from Brindisi, Italy to Patras, Greece (24-hour ride, several each day, free with Eurail). Do the Greek ruins, enjoy a vacation from your vacation in the sunny Isles, and fly home from Athens. (Open-jaws tickets into London and home from Athens are reasonable. This tour is ideal for a 21-day Eurailpass.)

My new *Great Britain in 22 Days*, *Spain and Portugal in 22 Days* and *Germany, Switzerland and Austria in 22 Days* books offer a tempting way to double—or triple—your vacation game plan.

You could also fly in and out of Frankfurt, using Rothenburg as your first night and St. Goar as your last.

To make the trip shorter and easier (15 days) skip Italy, going from Austria to Switzerland.

Many cheap flights connect the USA and Frankfurt. You could easily start your tour here, picking up a rental car or catching a train at the Frankfurt airport (it has a train station), going to Rothenburg (a great first-night-in-Europe place), and finishing three weeks later with a pleasant day on the Rhine within 2 or 3 hours of the airport and your flight home. Don't sleep in Frankfurt, just train into its station and catch the easy shuttle train service from there to the airport.

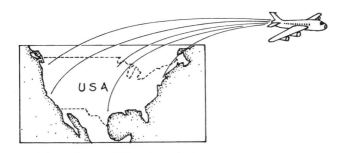

DAY 1
DEPART USA—AMSTERDAM

Call before going to the airport to confirm departure time as scheduled. Expect delays. Bring something to do—a book, a journal, some handwork—to make any waits easy on yourself. Remember, no matter how long it takes, flying to Europe is a very easy way to get there.

To minimize jet lag (body clock adjustment, stress):

■ Leave well rested. Pretend you are leaving a day earlier than you really are. Plan accordingly and enjoy a peaceful last day.

■ During the flight minimize stress by eating lightly, avoiding alcohol, caffeine and sugar. Drink juice.

■ Sleep through the in-flight movie—or at least close your eyes and fake it.

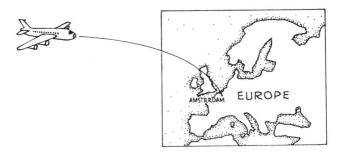

DAY 2
ARRIVE IN AMSTERDAM!

When flying to Europe, you usually land the next day. Amsterdam's Schiphol Airport (7 miles out of town and below sea level) is very efficient and "user friendly." Like nearly every European airport, it has a bank that keeps long hours and offers fair rates. There is also an information desk, plus baggage lockers, on-the-spot car rental agencies, an expensive room-finding service, and easy transportation service into the city. Airport taxis are expensive. Go by bus or train. The airport has a train station of its own. (You can validate your Eurailpass and hit the rails immediately, or pay to get into Amsterdam and start it later.)

If you're heading for central Amsterdam, catch a train ($1, leaving every 15 minutes); for Haarlem catch bus #174 or 176 from just behind the airport train station; for Delft and points south, the train is best—but explore your options at the information desk. Transportation in Holland is great. Buses will take you where trains don't and bicycles will take you where buses don't. Buses and trains both leave from train stations (where you can also rent bikes).

Around Amsterdam

The Netherlands

■ 13,000 square miles (Maryland's size).

■ 14 million people (1050 per square mile, compared to 58 per square mile in the USA).

■ The Netherlands, Europe's most densely populated country, is also one of its wealthiest and best organized. Efficiency is a local custom. The average income is higher than America's. Forty percent of the work force works with raw materials or in food processing while only 8 percent are farmers. Seventy percent of the land is cultivated, and you'll travel through vast fields of barley, wheat, sugar beets and potatoes.

■ Holland is the largest of 12 states which make up the Netherlands. Belgium, the Netherlands, and Luxembourg have united economically to form Benelux. Today you'll find no borders between these "Low Countries" —called that because they're low. Fifty percent of the Netherlands is below sea level, on land that has been reclaimed from the sea. That's why locals say, "God made the Earth but the Dutch made Holland." Modern technology and plenty of Dutch energy are turning more and more of the sea into fertile farm land.

The Dutch are easy-going, friendly and generally speak very good English. Dutch cities traditionally have been open-minded, loose and liberal, but they are now paying the price of this easy-going style. Amsterdam has become a bit seedy for many travelers' tastes. I enjoy more sedate Dutch evenings by sleeping in a small town nearby and side-tripping into the big city.

The best "Dutch" food is Indonesian (a former colony). Find any "Indish" restaurant and experience a rijstafel (rice table) which may have as many as 30 exciting dishes. Local taste treats are cheese, pancakes (pannekoeken), Dutch gin (jenever, pronounced like "your neighbor"), beer and "syrup waffles." Yogurt in Holland (and throughout Europe) is delicious and can be drunk right out of its plastic container. Breakfasts are big by Continental standards. Lunch and dinner are served at USA times.

The country is so small, level and well-covered by trains and buses that transportation is a snap. The excellent train and bus system attracts many visitors. Amsterdam, Rotterdam and The Hague are connected by speedy trains that come and go every 10 or 15 minutes. All you need to enjoy a driving vacation here is a car, gas and a map.

The Netherlands is a bicyclist's delight. The Dutch average four bikes per family, and have put a small bike road beside every big auto route. You can rent bikes at most train stations and drop them off at most other stations. Shops and banks stay open from 9 am to 5 pm. The industrious Dutch know no siesta.

The Netherlands

Delft: Small-town Headquarters for Holland

Delft, peaceful as a Vermeer painting (he was born there) and
lovely as the porcelain it makes, is a safe, pleasant and very comfortable place to overcome jet lag and break into Holland and
Europe. Delft is just 60 minutes by train from Amsterdam.
Trains depart every half hour, and cost about $8 round trip.
While Delft lacks major sights, it is a typically Dutch town with
a special soul. You'll enjoy it best just wandering around, watching people, munching, or gazing from the canal bridges into the
water and seeing the ripples play games with your face. The
town bustles during its Saturday morning market, and also has a
great Tuesday market which attracts many traditional villagers.
A town-wide sound system fills the colorful streets with pleasant music to browse by.

Food and Lodging

Believe me, you don't need to make reservations before you go.
Just drop in or call from the airport. Delft has several simple
hotels on its market square, the best being **Hotel Monopole**
(Tel. 015-123059. Say hi to Luke. $28 doubles with breakfast;
Luke also serves 56 varieties of pancakes. Address: Markt, Delft.)

I sleep at **Hotel Central** (Wijnhaven 6, 2611 CR, Delft, tel.
015-123442. It runs about $12 per person, with buffet breakfast,
showers, sauna; located between station and square.)

The **Peking** Chinese-Indonesian restaurant (2 minutes off

square, tel. 015-141100) serves a grand rijstafel Indonesian feast for about $5. A meal for two could stuff three hungry loggers.

Helpful Hints
Remember, if you're returning to Delft at the end of your trip, reserve a room in your favorite hotel. You can leave any un-needed luggage there free until you return. The free Delft porcelain tour is very interesting as are many sights in The Hague nearby (Madurodam—"mini Holland"—for kids; Torture museum—for parents traveling with kids; the world peace palace; and the Dutch "Coney Island" at nearby Scheveningen, which also has Holland's best Indonesian restaurant, the Bali).

    Haarlem: Like Delft, Haarlem is a fine small town home base for Holland. Haarlem is very close to both Amsterdam and the airport. **Hotel Carillon** (Grote Market 27, Haarlem, tel. 023-310591) is a fine place. It's $14 per person with breakfast, on the main square. Franz, who runs the place, speaks English and will hold a room until 4:00 p.m. with no deposit. Call him up.

    The Haarlem tourist info office (VVV) at the station is open from 9:00 to 6:00. For your rijstafel feast eat at the friendly Chinese-Indish restaurant **Nanking** (Kruisstraat 16, tel. 023/320706; the two-person dinner is plenty for three, $15). Also try the **Pannekoekhuis "De Smikkel"'** (Kruisweg 57, Hoek Parklaan, speaks English, cheery, dinner and dessert pancakes $4, closes at 8:00 p.m.) or eat at **St. Vincentius** on Nieuwe Greenmarket for cheap lunches and dinners. The **Nouveau Cafe**, 30 yards from Hotel Carillon, is a good place to try a jenever. For a taxi to the airport call 023-323000.

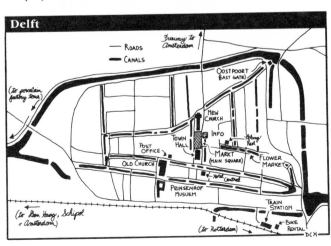

DAY 3
AMSTERDAM

While Amsterdam has grown a bit "seedy" for many people,
it is still worth a full day of sightseeing on even the busiest
itinerary. The central train station is your starting point (great
tourist information, bike rental, trains to all points) and Damrak
is the "main street" axis leading to the Dam Square (people-
watching and hang-out center) and to the Royal Palace. The
city's major sights are within walking distance of the Dam
Square. "Amsterdam in a day" is, if not thorough, very exciting.
Plan your time carefully, have a big breakfast and go for it.
You'll sleep good that night.

Suggested Schedule	
9:00 am	Anne Frank House, Westerkerk.
10:00 am	Palace, Dam Square, walk to Spui on Kalverstraat, Amsterdam's bustling pedestrian-only shopping street. Visit the Begijnhof.
Noon	Lunch, possible picnic.
1:00-5:00 pm	Museums. Divide your time between Rijks, Van Gogh and Stedelijk (modern art) museums, according to your interest.
5:00 pm	Walk through leidseplein (night club center) to Muntplein (flower market along canal) to Spui. Catch the hour-long canal boat tour.
7:00 pm	Walk past Dam Square, through red light district and sailors' quarters, possibly stopping for Indonesian dinner on Bantammerstraat, and back to the central station.

As you can—or will—see, Amsterdam and environs could
easily fill a second day.

Sightseeing Highlights
▲▲▲**Rijksmuseum**—Start visit with free, short slide show on
Dutch art (every 20 minutes all day). Great Rembrandts. Buy the
cheap museum map and plan your attack. Bookshop has good
posters, prints, slides and handy theme charts to the museum.
If you plan on collecting posters, buy a cardboard tube here.
There is also a cafeteria and w.c. (Tues-Sat 10-5, Sun 1-5)
▲▲▲**Van Gogh Museum**—Next to Rijksmuseum. Outstand-
ing. Beautifully displayed collection of Vincent's work. Don't
miss it. (Tues-Sat 10-5, Sun 1-5)

Stedelijk Modern Art Museum—Far-out art. Next to Van Gogh. Fun and refreshing. (Open Mondays also.)

▲▲**Anne Frank House**—A fascinating look at the hideaway where young Anne hid when the Nazis occupied the Netherlands. Pick up the English pamphlet at the door and don't miss the thought-provoking Neo-Nazi exhibit in the last room. Fascism is unfortunately not dead. (Mon-Sat 9-5, Sun 10-5)

Royal Palace interior.

Westerkerk—Important old church with Amsterdam's tallest steeple, worth climbing for the view. (Be careful: on a hot day Amsterdam's rooftops sprout nude sun worshippers.) Next to Anne Frank's.

▲▲**Canal Boat Tour**—Boats leave (constantly, everywhere) for the 90-minute, $3 introduction to the city. A good relaxing orientation. Bring a camera. No fishing.

Begijnhof—A tiny, idyllic courtyard in the city center where the Pilgrims worshipped and the charm of old Amsterdam can still be felt. Just off Kalverstraat between #130 and 132. The fine Amsterdam historical museum is just next door.

Rembrandt's House—Interesting for his fans. Lots of sketches.

Shopping—Waterlooplein (flea market), various flower markets, diamond dealers (free tours). Best walking/shopping street is parallel to Damrak.

Heineken Brewery Tours—Crowded, morning only. (9:00 & 11:00).

Red Light District—Europe's most interesting. Near station. Dangerous at night.

▲▲**Rent a Bike**—Around $2 a day, quick and easy at central train station (left end as you leave). Fly through the city with ease (suggested bike tour available at tourist information office). In one day I biked: through red light district, to Our Lord in the Attic (hidden church), to Herrengracht Mansion (at Herrengracht 605, typical old rich household), to Albert Cuypstraat Market (colorful daily street market), to a diamond polishing exhibit and tour (representing many companies), through Vondelpark (Amsterdam's "Central Park," good for people-watching and self-serve cafeteria lunch), to Jordaan district, to Anne Frank's, to Westerkerk (climbed tower), to Royal Palace, and down Damrak back to the station. Whew!

Food and Lodging

Good hotels are expensive. There's no shortage of simple hotels at $15 per person (see Arthur Frommer), student crash pads and hostels at $5 per night (see *Let's Go*). Room-finding service at tourist information offices can help but may steer you into more expensive places. Arrive early and find your own. By

afternoon the city can fill up. Best Indonesian restaurants are on Bantammerstraat. Try **Ling Nam** at #3 or **Azie** at #7, just east of the "sailor's quarters". Their Rice Table feast is $6-10.

Helpful Hints
Monday is a terrible day here. Museums are closed, and shops open only in the afternoon. Throughout the Netherlands, the VVV sign means tourist information. At tourist information office consider Falk map (best city map), "Amsterdam This Week" (periodical entertainment guide). "Use It" (student and hip guide) lists cheap beds, etc. The trolleys are great (six rides cost $2, or you can buy an all day pass for buses, trams and subway for $3.50. Get your tickets on your first ride.) If you get lost, just ride any one back to central train station. Drop by a bar for a jenever (Dutch gin)—the closest thing to an atomic bomb in a shot glass.

Side Trips
Many day tours are available from Amsterdam. buses go to villages from the station. It's important to see small-town Holland. The famous towns (Volendam, Marken Island, Edam, etc.) are very touristy but still fun. Zaandijk has the great Zaanse Schans, a 17th century Dutch village turned open-air folk museum where you can see and learn about cheese and

wooden-shoe making. Take an inspiring climb to the top of a whirring windmill (get a group of people together and ask for a short tour). You can even buy a small jar of fresh windmill-ground mustard for your next picnic. Zaandijk is a traveler's best one-stop look at traditional Dutch culture and includes the Netherlands' best collection of windmills. (Open daily 9-5, April through October, closed off-season. Ten miles north of Amsterdam, 15 minutes by train. Take the Alkmaar-bound train to Station Koog-Zaandijk and walk for 8 minutes. Free.) Alkmaar is Holland's cheese town—especially fun during its weekly market, Fridays from 10:00 to noon.

The energetic can enjoy a rented bicycle tour of the countryside. A free ferry departs from behind the station across the canal. In five minutes Amsterdam will be gone and you'll be rolling through the polderland.

The sleek rebuilt-since-the-war city of Arnhem has two wonderful attractions. Its open air folk museum (which rivals Bokrijk, a Belgian equivalent listed under Day 4) displays a great collection of traditional Dutch buildings, lifestyles and crafts. Nearby is the Hoge Veluwe National Park—Holland's largest—which is famous for its Kroller-Muller museum. This huge and impressive collection of modern art including 276 paintings by Van Gogh is set deep in this natural Dutch wilderness. The park has lots more to offer including hundreds of white-painted bikes you're free to use to make your explorations more fun. Ask any Dutch tourist office for more info on Arnhem and consider seeing its open air museum rather than Bokrijk on the road to the Rhine as described tomorrow. Arnhem lies one hour by car or train from Amsterdam on the way to the Rhineland.

DAY 4
FROM HOLLAND TO THE RHINE

Today's objective is to get to Germany's Rhineland in the most
interesting way. This will be your first European border
crossing.

Suggested Schedule

8:00 am	Drive from Delft or Haarlem to Bokrijk.
11:00 am	Lunch and tour open-air folk museum.
2:00 pm	Drive to St. Goar on the Rhine with an hour stop in Boppard.
7:00 pm	Dinner at hotel.
9:00 pm	Evening in St. Goar

Transportation
By car from Delft, the most rewarding route is through the
northeast corner of Belgium (freeway nearly all the way), stopping between Hasselt and Genk to tour the Bokrijk Folk Museum.
(Amsterdam-Bokrijk: 3 hours, Bokrijk-St. Goar: 3 hours.)

Driving on you'll pass Aachen (Aix la Chapelle), Charlemagne's
capital city 1,200 years ago, and on into castle country. Follow
the signs into Koblenz where you'll cross the Mosel River into
town (see the Mosel on the right, the Deutches Ecke, where the
Rhine and Mosel meet, on the left). Follow signs to road #9 to
Mainz along the Rhine's west bank. As you leave town you'll see
the huge brewery of Koenigbrau and the yellow castle of
Stoltzenfels.

Boppard is worth a stop. Park near the center. Just above the
market square are the remains of a Roman wall. On the square,
buy the little Mainz-Koblenz guide book (4.50 DM) with map.
Below the square is a fascinating church. See carved Roman-
esque crazies at the doorway. Inside, notice the 1,500-year-old
Christian symbols on the wall to the right of the entrance and
the typical painted arches (remember, most old churches were
painted this way). On the arches near the river, note the high
water (*hoch wasser*) marks from various flood years. St.
Goar is just a few minutes upstream. Note Marksburg Castle (the
only castle on the Rhine not destroyed by the French) across
the river from the village of Spey—it makes a great photo. Hotel
Landsknecht is next to the Mercedes dealer one mile north of
St. Goar. Hotel Montag is just across from the world's biggest
cuckoo clock in the old town.

By train, Bokrijk isn't worth the trouble. Zaandijk is the best
substitute. Enjoy rural and village Holland for half a day, then
zip direct to Koblenz in 4 to 4½ hours, and on to St. Goar for
dinner. Or you can leave Amsterdam early and stop off in Koln
(Germany's greatest gothic cathedral, the impressive Romisch-
Germanisches museum and the tourist office are just across the
street from the station), Bonn (Germany's peaceful capital city,
with a great marketplace and the visit-worthy birthplace of
Beethoven), and historic Koblenz where the Rhine and Mosel
join forces. There are plenty of trains from Koblenz to St. Goar.
(Consider a short stop at Boppard en route.)

Bokrijk
This huge park in the Belgian province of Limburg boasts the
biggest and best open-air folk museum in all the Low Countries.
Entire villages—not just houses—from the Middle Ages have
been reassembled here so visitors can learn about the pillories,
thatched roofs, windmills and lifestyles of old. Try to get a guided tour. Otherwise, the fine English guidebook (75 BF) is your
key to understanding what you see.

Bokrijk has much more—including an old-fashioned
restaurant (next to the pillory) serving traditional meals (sample
some of Belgium's great beer—like Trappist), a zoo, rose
garden, nature reserve, youth hostel, and a great opportunity
to see Belgian families enjoying life's simple pleasures.

While Bokrijk is in Belgium, you won't even know when
you've crossed the border. Benelux has blurry borders. Dutch
money is accepted at Bokrijk.

Germany
■ 95,000 square miles (smaller than Oregon).
■ 65 million people (about 650 per square mile, and declining
slowly).
■ Ja, Deutschland. Energetic, efficient, organized and Europe's
economic muscleman. Eighty-five percent of its people live in
cities. Ninety-seven percent of the workers get a one-month
paid vacation, and during the other eleven months they create a
gross national product of about one-third the USA's. Germany is
the world's fifth biggest industrial power, ranking fourth in steel
output and nuclear power, third in automobile production. It
also shines culturally, beating out all but two countries in production of books, Nobel laureates and professors.
■ While northern Germany is Protestant and the populace
assaults life aggressively, southern Germany is Catholic, more
relaxed and leisurely. The southern German, or Bavarian,
dialect is to High (northern) German what the dialect of
Alabama or Georgia is to the northern USA.

Germany

■ Germany's most interesting tourist route today—Rhine, Romantic Road, Bavaria—was yesterday's most important trade route, where Germany's most prosperous and important medieval cities were located. Remember, Germany as a nation is just barely 100 years old. In 1850 there were 35 independent countries in what is now Germany. In medieval times there were over 300 independent little countries in Germany, each with its own weights, measures, coinage and king. Many were surrounded by what we call iron curtains. This helps explain the many diverse customs found in such a compact land.

■ Practice your German energetically because nearly half of this tour is in German-speaking countries (Germany, Austria, Switzerland).

■ Germans eat lunch from 12 pm-3 pm and dinner between 6 pm and 9 pm. Each region has its own gastronomic twist, so order local house specials in restaurants when possible. Fish and venison are good. Great beer and white wines are every-where. Try the small local brands. "Gummi Bears" are a local gumdrop candy with a cult following (beware of imitations—

you must see the word "Gummi"), and Nutella is a chocolate nut spread specialty that may change your life.
■ Banks are generally open 8 am-12:30 pm and 1:30 pm-4 pm, other offices from 8 am to 4 pm. August is a holiday month for workers—but that doesn't really affect us tourists.

Food and Lodging
The Rhineland has plenty of budget rooms (zimmers) and gasthauses offering fine rooms for $10 to $12 per person, including breakfast. St. Goar, Bacharach and a few other towns have hostels where you'll get a bed for $4. The St. Goar hostel, a big white building directly under the castle, is run very German-style. (Dinners cost about $5 in the small hotels, $3 at the hostel.) Spend the late evening in a winestube—soaking up the atmosphere, and some of the local Rhine wine.

I stay one mile north of St. Goar in the friendly riverside **Hotel Landsknecht** (tel. 06741-1693). Klaus Nickenig and family charge $35 per double with breakfast. Also good in town (easier for those without a car) is **Hotel Montag** (tel. 06741/1629, #128 Heerstrasse).

If you're staying in Oberwesel (another lovely Rhine village) stay at friendly Frau Maus' **Pension Huhn** at 39 Chablis Strasse. **Restaurant Zum Lamm** has great food and wine. (Note: German wines are labeled *suss* for sweet, with a red label; *halbtrocken* for semi-dry, with a green label; and *trocken* for dry, with a gold medallion.)

The town of Bacharach, near St. Goar, has Germany's best youth hostel—a castle on the hilltop with a royal Rhine view. In Bacharach I'd recommend **Hotel Kranenturm** for cheap, friendly accommodations and great cooking. Dinner at **Altes Haus**—the oldest building in town.

Side Trips
Nearby Aachen is a fun town. Charlemagne's ancient capital, it's one of Germany's most historic and underrated cities. Don't miss its unique newspaper museum.

The Mosel River, which joins the Rhine at Koblenz, is more pleasant and less industrial than the Rhine. Lined with vineyards, tempting villages and two exciting castles (Cochem and Berg Eltz), it's a fine place to spend an extra day if you have one. Cochem is the best home base for the Mosel region.

DAY 5
THE RHINE TO ROTHENBURG

Spend today exploring the Rhine's biggest castle, cruising down its most famous stretch and driving on to Rothenburg, Germany's best-preserved medieval town.

The banks open at 8 am in St. Goar. Change enough money to get you through Germany. The Rheinfels Castle is a 15-minute walk up the hill. (You can't miss it; it's the Rhine's biggest and most important castle.) Be there at 9 am when it opens. The castle has several miles of rather spooky tunnels under it (bring your flashlight). See if there's a guided tour available. The castle shop sells a beautifully illustrated children's book called "Father Rhine Tells His Sagas" ($5, big edition). The handiest guide book for this region is the small, red Mainz-Koblenz book with foldout Rhine map (less than $2).

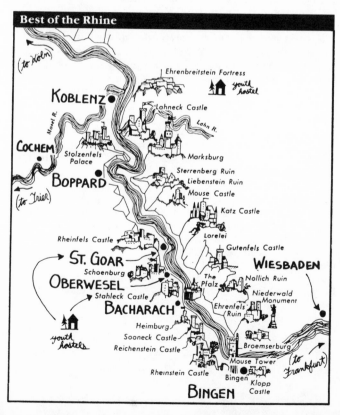

Best of the Rhine

Be back downtown at the Koln-Dusseldorfer boat dock to catch the 10:15 am boat to Bacharach—a one-hour ride upstream ($6 or free with Eurail. You should confirm departure time the night before, from your hotel. Buy your ticket at the dock at 10:10—it never fills up.) Sit on the top deck with your handy Rhine map-guide and enjoy the parade of castles, towns, boats and vineyards. You'll pass and hopefully survive the seductive Lorelei—the huge rock from which, according to highly placed legendary sources, a beautiful maiden once lured medieval boats onto the rocks. Any postcard rack will tell you the story in English.

At about 11:20 am you'll de-ship at Bacharach where, after a picnic (grocery shops in town) in the riverfront park, you'll continue on, by car or train (about one per hour), down the Rhine to Mainz (which has a great little museum about Gutenberg and the birth of printing) and then by autobahn on to Rothenburg.

Suggested Schedule	
7:30 am	Breakfast.
8:15 am	Banking and browsing in St. Goar.
9:00 am	Tour Rheinfels Castle.
10:15 am	Catch the Rhine steamer, cruise to Bacharach.
11:30 am	Free time for picnic lunch, tour of town.
1:00 pm	Drive to Rothenburg.
5:00 pm	Find hotel and get set up.
Evening	Free in Rothenburg.

Transportation
If you are driving, taking the boat ride can present a problem. You can (1) skip the boat, (2) take a round-trip tourist excursion boat ride from St. Goar, (3) let one person in your group drive to Bacharach, prepare the picnic and meet the boat, or (4) take the boat to Bacharach and return by train, spending your wait time exploring that old half-timbered town. I'd probably take the first option and spend more time poking around with the car. From Bacharach to Mainz are plenty of good castles. After that you can hit the autobahn, skirting Frankfurt and setting the auto-pilot on Wurzburg. You'll pass U.S. military bases, Europe's busiest airport and lots of trucks. At Wurzburg, take the small road south to Rothenburg, or if in a hurry, continue south on the new autobahn.

If you're traveling by train, your Eurailpass gets you onto the Rhine cruise and the Romantische Strasse (Romantic Road) bus tour free. The best hour-long cruise of the Rhine is from St. Goar to Bacharach (see the boat schedule in the back of this guide). If you're really enjoying the cruise, stay on to Wiesbaden. If you get off at Bacharach, hourly trains link Bacharach with St. Goar and Bingen. Ask for schedule information at the boat dock.

The Romantic Road bus tour leaves Wiesbaden at 7 am daily, and from the Frankfurt train station at 8:15. A reservation is advisable only on summer weekends. Just telephone 069-7903240 three days in advance (you can arrange for an overnight stopover in Rothenburg). You can train to Rothenburg. This is tricky and takes about three hours: Frankfurt to Wurzburg (many trains), Wurzburg to Steinach (hourly), Steinach to Rothenburg (almost hourly). Get specifics at any German station. Enjoy an evening in that most romantic of medieval German towns and catch the same bus on to Munich or Fussen 24 hours later (see the schedule in the back pages).

While the Rhine is fine by boat, car and train, it also has a great riverside bicycle path, and it is possible to rent and return bikes at different train stations. This part of the Rhine has no bridges, but plenty of ferries.

Food and Lodging

Rothenburg is crowded with visitors (including what is probably Europe's greatest single concentration of Japanese tourists), but finding a room is no problem. From the main square (which has a tourist office with room-finding service), just walk downhill on Schmiedgasse street until it becomes Spitalgasse. This street has plenty of gasthauses, zimmers ($10 per person with breakfast) and two fine $3-a-night youth hostels (Jugendherberge in German, tel. 09861-4510.) I stay in #28, **Hotel Goldene Rose**, tel. 09861-4638 for about $12 a night. Less expensive yet and very friendly is a room in the home of **Herr Moser** on Spitalgasse #12 (tel. 5971). Also good are **Gastehaus Raidel** (Wenggasse 3, tel. 3115), **Pension Poschel** (Wengasse 22, tel. 3430) and **Pension Becker** (Rosengasse 23, tel. 5562).

Itinerary Option

Wurzburg—An easy two-hour side trip (30 minutes in and out, 1 hour sightseeing) is to visit Wurzburg's Prince Bishop's residence, the "Versailles" of Franconia, with a lavish Baroque chapel—take the Heidingsfield-Wurzburg exit and follow the signs to Wurzburg's "stadtmitte, centrum" and then to the Residenz (ask). Open till 5, last entrance at 4:30. Buy a guidebook, or try to latch onto an English tour. If you have time, the Marienburg fortress houses a fascinating Franconian folk museum with lots of Riemenschneider carvings. To leave, follow autobahn Nuremberg signs.

DAY 6
ROTHENBURG OB DER TAUBER

Rothenburg is well worth two nights and a whole day. In the Middle Ages, when Frankfurt and Munich were just wide spots in the road, Rothenburg had a whopping population of 6,000. It was Germany's second largest city. Today it's her best-preserved medieval walled town, enjoying tremendous tourist popularity without losing its charm.

Too often Rothenburg brings out the shopper in visitors, before they have had a chance to appreciate the historic city. True, this is a great place to do your German shopping, but first see the town. The tourist information office on the market square has guided tours in English. If none are scheduled, hire a private guide. For about $25, a local historian—who's usually an intriguing character as well—will bring the ramparts alive. A thousand years of history is packed between the cobbles. Call Karen Bierstedt (09861-2217) or Manfred Baumann (4146).

Sightseeing Highlights
First, pick up a map and information at tourist information office on main square (9:00-6:00, Sat 9:00-12:00, Closed Sunday).

Confirm sightseeing plans and ask about the daily 1:30 walking tours and evening entertainment. Tel. 40492.

To orient yourself, think of the town map as a head. Its nose, the castle, sticks out to the left, the neck is the lower panhandle part (with the youth hostels and my favorite hotel).

▲**Walk the Wall**—1½ miles around, great views, good orientation. Can be done speedily in one hour. Photographers will go through lots of film. Ideal before breakfast, or at sunset.

▲▲**Climb Town Hall Tower**—Best view of town and surrounding countryside. (9:30-12:30, 1-5. 1DM). Rigorous but interesting climb.

▲▲**Medieval Crime and Punishment Museum**—This is the best of its kind, full of fascinating old legal bits and pieces, instruments of punishment and torture, even a special cage—complete with a metal gag—for nags. Exhibits in English. Open 9:30-7, $2

▲▲▲**St. Jacob's Church**—Here you'll find the best Riemenschneider altar-piece, dated 1466, located up the stairs and behind the organ. Riemenschneider was the Michelangelo of German woodcarvers. This is the one "must see" art treasure in town. Open daily 9:30-5:30, Sun 10:30-5:30, $1.

Be in the main square at 11 am, 12 pm, 1, 2, 3, 9 or 10 pm— for the ritual gathering of the tourists to see the breathtaking reenactment of the Meistertrunk story. You'll learn about the town's most popular legend, a fun, if fanciful, story.

▲**Walk in the countryside**—Just below the Burggarten (castle garden) in the Tauber Valley is the cute, skinny 600-year-old castle/summer home of Mayor Toppler (open 10-12, 2-5). It's furnished intimately and is well worth a look. Notice the photo of bombed out 1945 Rothenburg on the top floor.

Across from the castle, a radiantly happy lady will show you her 800-year-old water-powered flour mill called the Fuchsmuhle. Down the road check out the covered bridges and the many big trout. Complete your countryside stroll by walking to the little village of Detwang. It is actually older than Rothenburg and has another fine Riemenschneider altarpiece and a great local-style restaurant next to its campground. The most direct path from Rothenburg to Detwang is from the Klingentor Gate. The sunsets over the "Tauber Riviera" and from the Berggarten Park are wonderful.

DAY 7
ROMANTIC ROAD TO TYROL

Get an early start to enjoy the quaint hills and rolling villages of this romantic region. What was long ago Germany's major medieval trade route is today's top tourist trip. Drive through cute Dinkelsbuhl and continue south, crossing the baby Danube River (Donau in German) to Dachau. Explore the concentration camp and drive through the rest of Bavaria (a short stop in Munich makes your day more exciting—and complicated) to Reutte (pronounced "roy-tah") in Tyrol, Austria, to make your home base for tomorrow's "castle day" and Bavarian explorations.

Suggested Schedule

7:30 am	Breakfast.
8:00 am	Drive south on Romantic Road.
11:00 am	Tour Dachau.
1:00 pm	Drive to Austria with possible stop in Munich.
5:00 pm	Arrive in Reutte.
7:00 pm	Dinner.
8:30 pm	Tyrolian Folk Evening.

Transportation
By car you'll be following the green "Romantische Strasse" signs, winding scenically through the small towns until you hit the autobahn near Augsburg. Take the autobahn towards Munich ("Munchen") exiting at Dachau. Now follow the signs marked "KZ Gedenkstatte." After Dachau, avoid the Munich traffic by crossing back over the autobahn and heading for Furstenfeld, then Inning, then Landsberg and on to Fussen. If the weather's good, drive by Neuschwanstein castle. Just over the border in Austria, you'll find Reutte.

If you want to swing into Munich, follow the Dachauerstrasse from Dachau right downtown. You'll see the Olympic Stadium at the base of the huge TV tower. Parking is easy there—and you can take the U-Bahn (subway) downtown to Marianplatz. An hour around this central square gives you a good feel for this booming and very human city.

By train pass, catch the Romantic Road bus tour from the Rothenburg train station (or from the parkplatz at the north end of town). Two buses come through in the early afternoon. You can catch one bus into Munich (arrives at 6:55 pm) or the other direct to Fussen (arrives at 7:55 pm). Ask about reservations and

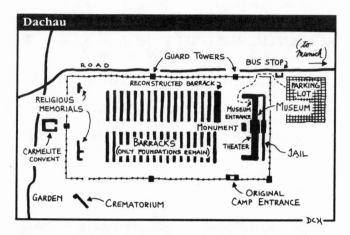

exact times in Rothenburg at the train station or tourist office.
Be early. If you stake out a seat when the bus arrives you'll have
a better chance of being on it when it leaves two hours later.

Dachau
Dachau was the first Nazi concentration camp (1933). Today it
is the most accessible camp to travelers and is a very effective
voice from our recent but grisly past, warning and pleading
"Never Again"—the memorial's theme. This is a valuable experience, and when approached thoughtfully is well worth the
drive—in fact, it may change your life. See it. Feel it. Read and
think about it. After this most powerful sightseeing experience,
many people gain a respect for history and are inspired to learn
more about contemporary injustices, and work against tragic
reoccurrences.

Upon arrival, pick up the mini-guide and notice when the
next documentary film in English will be shown (normally
11:30). The museum and the movie are worthwhile. Notice the
expressionist Fascist-inspired art near the theater. Outside, be
sure to tour the reconstructed barracks and the memorial
shrines at the far end. (Near the theater are English books, slides
and a good w.c. The camp is open 9 am-5 pm, closed on
Mondays.)

Food and Lodging
In July and August Munich and Bavaria are packed with tourists.
Tyrol in Austria is easier and a bit cheaper. Reutte is just one of
many good home base towns in the area. I choose it because it's

not so crowded in peak season, the easy-going locals are always in a party mood, and I like to stay overnight in Austria. Reutte has a good little youth hostel (tel. 05672-3039; follow the Jugendherberg signs from the town center, a 5-minute walk, non-members accepted, clean, rarely full, friendly, open only June 15-Aug 25), and plenty of reasonable hotels and zimmers. I stay at the big, central **Hotel Goldener Hirsch** (from Germany dial 0043-5672-2508, in Reutte just the last four digits; ask for Helmut or Monika) which charges $18 per person and serves great $5 dinners. The Reutte tourist office, one block in front of the station, open 'til 6:00 daily, can always find you a $7 bed in a private home.

In Munich there's a helpful room-finding service in the train station's tourist information office (open Mon-Sat 8:00 am-11:00 pm, Sun 1:00-9:30 pm, tel. 239-1259). They can usually find you a reasonable room near the station. In Oberammergau I enjoyed friendly budget accommodations and hearty cooking at the **Gasthaus zum Stern** (Dorfstrasse 33, 8103 Oberammergau, tel. 08822-867). Oberammergau's youth hostel is un-friendly but very good in all other ways (tel. 08822-4114). Countryside guest houses abound in Bavaria and are a great value. Look for signs that say "zimmer frei." The going rate is 42 DM ($20) per double including breakfast.

Itinerary Options

To save a day you could see Rothenburg during the Romantic

Romantische Strasse

road tour lunch stop and continue south. Munich is a cultural center, capital of Bavaria, and is well worth at least a day if you have the time.

Austria

■ 32,000 square miles (South Carolina's size).
■ 7.6 million people (235 per square mile and holding).
■ Austria during the grand old Hapsburg days, was Europe's most powerful empire. Its royalty put together that giant empire of more than 50 million people by making love, not war (having lots of children and marrying them into the other royal houses of Europe).
■ Today Austria is a small landlocked country that does more to cling to its elegant past than any other in Europe. The waltz is still the rage and Austrians are very sociable. More so than anywhere else, it's important to greet people you pass on the streets or meet in shops. The Austrian's version of Hi is a cheerful "Gruss, Gott!" (May God greet you). You'll get the correct pronunciation after the first volley—listen and copy.
■ While they speak German and German money is readily accepted in Salzburg, Innsbruck and Reutte, the Austrians cherish their distinct cultural and historical traditions. They are not Germans. Austria is mellow and relaxed compared to Deutschland. *Gemutlichkeit* is the German word for this special Austrian cozy-and-easy approach to life. It's good living—either engulfed in mountain beauty or lavish high culture. The people like to stroll as if every day were Sunday, topping things off with a visit to a coffee or pastry shop. It must be nice to be past your prime—no longer troubled by being powerful, able to kick back and enjoy just being happy in the clean, untroubled mountain air. While the Austrians make less money than their neighbors, they work less (34 hours a week) and live longer (14 percent of the people are senior citizens, the highest percentage in the world). Austria is technically part of Eastern Europe and therefore not in NATO or the EEC.
■ Austrians eat on about the same schedule as we do. Treats include Wiener Schnitzel (breaded veal cutlet), Knodel (dumplings), Apfelstrudel and fancy deserts. White wines, Heurigen (new wine) and coffee are delicious and popular. Shops are open from 8 am to 5 pm. Banks keep roughly the same hours, but usually close for lunch.

DAY 8

BAVARIA AND CASTLE DAY

Our goal today is to explore two very different castles, Germany's finest Rococo-style church, and a typical Bavarian village. We'll make a circular tour starting in Reutte.

Suggested Schedule

7:30 am	Breakfast.
8:15 am	Leave Reutte.
8:30 am	Neuschwanstein, tour Ludwig's castle.
11:30 am	Picnic lunch.
12:15 pm	Drive to Wies church (20-minute stop) and on to Oberammergau.
1:45 pm	Tour Oberammergau or Linderhof castle.
3:15 pm	Drive back into Austria via Garmish and the Zugspitz.
4:30 pm	Sommerrodelbahn (luge) ride in Lermoos.
6:00 pm	Hike to ruined castle.
7:30 pm	Dinner in Reutte.
8:30 pm	Tyrol folk evening (if not last night).

Transportation and Sightseeing Highlights

This day is designed for drivers. Without your own wheels it won't be possible. Local buses serve the area—but not very well. Buses from Fussen station to Neuschwanstein run hourly, $1; Fussen-Wies, twice a day for $3; Oberammergau-Linderhof, fairly regularly. Hitchhiking is possible, but instead I'd take an all-day bus tour from Munich to cover these sights most efficiently.

It's best to see Neuschwanstein, Germany's most popular castle, early in the morning before the hordes hit. The castle is open every morning at 8:30 am. By 10 am it's packed. Hiking up the steep road to the castle you may pass a crazy old bearded Bavarian. (Hug him if you like, he's a photographer's feast, but women beware of his infamous sauerkraut tongue.) Take the English tour and learn the story of Bavaria's Mad King Ludwig. (The tour is bare-bones and usually rushed. If possible, read up on Wagner's operas and Ludwig's life before your visit.)

After the tour, if you are energetic, climb up to Mary's Bridge for a great view of Europe's "Disney" castle. The big yellow more "lived-in" Hohenschwangau castle nearby was Ludwig's boyhood home. Like its more exciting neighbor, it costs about

Bavarian Tyrolean Loop

$3 and takes about an hour to tour.

Back down in the village you'll find several restaurants. The Jagerhaus is by far the cheapest, with food that tastes that way. Next door is a handy little grocery store. Picnic in the lakeside park. At the intersection you'll find the best gift shop (with fine manger scenes and Hummels much cheaper than in Rothenburg), the bus stop, international dial-direct-to-home phone booths (001-pause-area code-your number. Plug in one Deutsch Mark for 15 seconds of hometown gossip.).

Just north of Neuschwanstein is the Tegelberg gondola. For $5 it will carry you high above the castle to that peak's 5,500-foot summit. On a clear day you get great views of the Alps and Bavaria and the thrill of watching hang gliders leap into airborne ecstasy. From there it's a lovely 2-hour hike to Ludwig's castle. Tegelberg has a mountain hut with Tolkien atmosphere and $5 beds, if you'd like to spend the night and do Ludwig's place the next morning. (Last ride, 5 pm.)

Germany's greatest Rococo-style church, Wies Church, is bursting with beauty just 30 minutes down the road. Go north, turn right at Steingaden, and follow the signs. This church is a droplet of heaven, a curly curlicue, the final flowering of the Baroque movement. Read about it as you sit in its splendor, then walk back to the car park the long way, through the meadow.

Oberammergau, the Shirley Temple of Bavarian villages and exploited to the hilt by the tourist trade, has a resilient charm. It's worth a wander. Browse through the wood carver's shops— small art galleries filled with very expensive whittled works. Visit the church, a cousin of the Wies. Tour the great Passion Play theater (30 minutes, $1, throughout the day). And get out.

From Oberammergau drive through Garmish, past Germany's highest mountain, the Zugspitz, into Austria via Lermoos.

Or you can take the small scenic road past Ludwig's Linderhof Castle. It's the most liveable palace I've seen. Incredible grandeur on a homey scale and worth a look if you have the energy and two hours for the tour. Wind past the windsurfer-strewn Plansee, and back into Austria.

The Fernpass road from Reutte to Innsbruck passes the ruined castles of Ehrenberg (just outside of town) and two exciting luge courses. The first course is a ten minute drive beyond the ruins. Look for a chairlift on the right side of the road. In the summer, this ski slope is used as a luge course, "Sommerrodel-bahn" in German. It's one of Europe's great $2 thrills: take the lift up, grab a sled-like go-cart and luge down. The concrete bobsled course banks on the corners and even a novice can go very, very fast. No one emerges from the course without a windblown hairdo and a smile-creased face. (Closed at 5:00 and when raining.) Twenty minutes further toward Innsbruck , just past Lermoos (the first exit after a long tunnel) is a better luge, the longest in Austria—4,000 feet. It opens at 8:30 am—a good tomorrow morning alternative if today is wet.

The brooding ruins of Ehrenberg await survivors of the luge. These are a great contrast after this morning's modern castles. Park in the lot at the base of the hill and hike up. It's a 20-minute walk to the small castle, for a great view from your own private

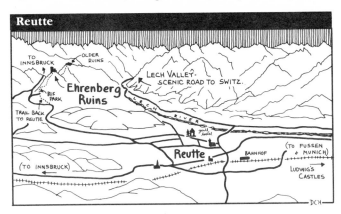

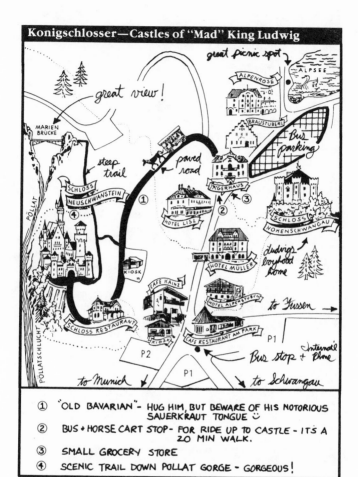

Konigschlosser—Castles of "Mad" King Ludwig

① "OLD BAVARIAN" - HUG HIM, BUT BEWARE OF HIS NOTORIOUS SAUERKRAUT TONGUE ☺
② BUS & HORSE CART STOP - FOR RIDE UP TO CASTLE - IT'S A 20 MIN WALK.
③ SMALL GROCERY STORE
④ SCENIC TRAIL DOWN POLLAT GORGE - GORGEOUS!

ruins. For more castle mystique climb 30 minutes up the neighboring taller hill. Its ruined castle is bigger, more desolate and overgrown, more romantic. The easiest way down is via the small road from the gulley between the two castles. Reutte is a pleasant walk away.

Itinerary Options
Train travelers may prefer spending this time in Munich and in Salzburg (two hours apart by hourly train). Salzburg holds its own against "castle day" and is better than Innsbruck. Consider a side trip to Salzburg from Munich and the night train from Munich to Venice.

DAY 9
DRIVE OVER THE ALPS TO VENICE

Innsbruck, Western Austria's major city and just a scenic hour's drive from Reutte, is a great place to spend the morning. Park as centrally as possible and give yourself three hours to see the town center and have a picnic lunch. Then it's on to Italy. Italy is a whole new world. Now it's time for sunshine, cappucino, gelato and *la dolce vita*!

Suggested Schedule

8:00 am	Drive from Reutte to Innsbruck.
9:30 am	Sightseeing in downtown Innsbruck, lunch.
12:30 pm	Drive from Innsbruck to Venice.
5:30 pm	Take boat #1, the slow boat, down the Grand Canal to San Marco. Find your hotel.

Sightseeing Hints—Innsbruck
The Golden Roof is the historic center of town. From this square you'll see a tourist information booth with maps and lists of sights, the newly restored Baroque-style Helblinghaus, the city tower (climb it for a great view), and the new Olympics museum with exciting action videos for winter sports lovers.

Nearby are the palace (Hofburg) and church and the very important Tyroler Volkskunst Museum. This museum ($1, open 9-5 daily, closed Sunday afternoons) is the best look anywhere at traditional Tyrolian lifestyles, with fascinating exhibits ranging from wedding dresses and babies' cribs to nativity scenes. Use the helpful English guidebook ($2).

A very popular mountain sports center and home of the 1964 and 1976 Winter Olympics, Innsbruck is surrounded by 150 mountain lifts, 1,250 miles of trails and 250 hikers' huts. If it's sunny, consider taking the lift right out of the city to the mountaintops above.

After lunch drive south over the dramatic Brenner Pass. The autobahn Europa Bridge costs $6 more than the old road, but will save you enough gas, time and nausea to be worthwhile. This four-hour drive takes you through beautiful Italian mountains, past countless castles, around Romeo and Juliet's hometown of Verona and on to Venice. It's *autostrada* (superhighway—with tolls) all the way.

Italy
■ 116,000 square miles (the size of Arizona).
■ 56,000,000 people (477 per square mile).

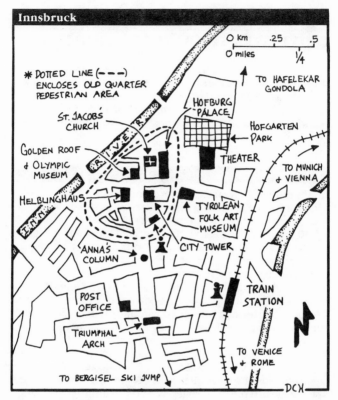

Innsbruck

* DOTTED LINE (— — —)
ENCLOSES OLD QUARTER
PEDESTRIAN AREA

St. JACOBS CHURCH

GOLDEN ROOF & OLYMPIC MUSEUM

HELBLINGHAUS

ANNA'S COLUMN

POST OFFICE

TRIUMPHAL ARCH

TO BERGISEL SKI JUMP

HOFBURG PALACE

HOFGARTEN PARK

THEATER

TYROLEAN FOLK ART MUSEUM

CITY TOWER

TRAIN STATION

TO HAFELEKAR GONDOLA

TO MUNICH & VIENNA

TO VENICE & ROME

0 km   .25   .5
0 miles   ¼

—DCH—

■ Ah, Italy! It has Europe's richest, craziest culture—if I had to
choose just one. Italy is a blast, if you take it on its terms and accept the package deal. Some people, often with considerable ef-
fort, manage to hate it. Italy bubbles with emotion, corruption,
inflation, traffic jams, strikes, rallies, holidays, crowded squalor
and irate ranters shaking their fists at each other one minute and
walking arm in arm the next. Have a talk with yourself before
you cross the border. Promise yourself to relax, and soak in it.
It's a glorious mud puddle. Be militantly positive.
■ With so much history and art in Venice, Florence and Rome,
you'll need to be a student here to maximize your experience.
Italy has two basic halves. the north is relatively industrial, ag-
gressive and time-is-money in its outlook. The Po River basin
and the area between Milan, Genoa and Torino is the richest
farmland and the industrial heartland. The south is more
crowded, poor, relaxed, farm-oriented and traditional. Families
here are very strong and usually live in the same house for many

generations. Loyalties are to the family, city, region, then country—in that order. The Apennine Mountains give Italy a rugged north-south spine.

■ Economically, Italy has its problems but things somehow work out. Statistically it looks terrible (high inflation, a low average income) but things work wonderfully under the table. Italy is a leading wine producer and is sixth in the world in cheese and wool output. Tourism (your dollars) is a big part of the economy.

■ Italy, home of the Vatican, is Catholic but the dominant religion is soccer—especially since their World Cup championship in 1982.

■ The language is easy. Be melodramatic and move your hand with your tongue. Hear the melody, get into the flow. Fake it, let the farce be with you. Italians are outgoing characters. They want to communicate and try harder than any other Europeans. Play with them.

■ Italy, a land of extremes, is also the most thief-ridden country you'll visit. Tourists suffer virtually no violent crime—just petty purse-snatchings, pick-pocketings and short-changings. Only the sloppy will be stung. Wear your moneybelt! Count your change.

■ Traditionally, Italy works on the siesta plan: from 8 or 9 am to 1 pm and from 3:30 pm to 7 pm, six days a week. Many businesses have adopted the government's new recommended 8 am-2 pm work day. In tourist areas, shops are open longer.

■ Sightseeing hours are always changing in Italy and many of the hours in this book will be wrong by the time you travel. Use

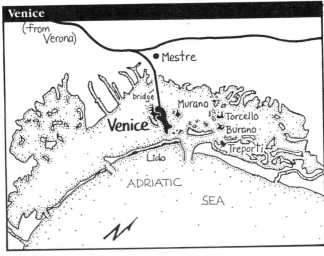

Italy

the tourist offices to double-check your sightseeing plans.
■ Many Italian churches require modest dress—no shorts or
bare shoulders.
■ The Italian autostrada is lined with Europe's best rest stops,
with gas, coffee bars, w.c.'s, long distance telephones, grocery
stores, restaurants and often change facilities and tourist info.
■ While no longer a cheap country, Italy is still a hit with shop-
pers. Glassware (Venice), gold, silver, leather and prints
(Florence) and high fashion (Rome) are good souvenirs.
■ Many tourists are mind-boggled by the huge price figures:
16,000 lire for dinner! 42,000 for the room! 126,000 for the taxi
ride! That's still real money—it's just spoken of in much smaller
units than a dollar. Since there are roughly 1,500 lire in a dollar
(at this writing), figure Italian lire prices by covering the last
three zeros with your finger and taking two-thirds of the re-
maining figure. So that 16,000-lire dinner costs $10 in U.S.
money, the room $28, and the taxi ride . . . oh oh!
■ Italians eat a miniscule breakfast, a huge lunch between
12:30 pm and 3:30 pm and a light dinner (quite late). Food in
Italy is given great importance and should be thought of as
"sightseeing for your tongue." Focus on regional specialties,
wines, and pastas. In restaurants you'll be billed a cover charge
(*coperto*) and a 10-15% service charge. A salad minestrone and
pasta, while not a proper meal, is cheaper, more fun and plenty

of food. The gelati (ice cream) and the coffee are the best anywhere. Have fun in the bars, explore the menus. Bar procedure can be frustrating. Decide what you want, check the price list on the wall, pay the cashier, give the receipt to the bartender and tell him what you want.

■ *La Dolce Far Niente!* (The sweetness of doing nothing!) is a big part of Italy. Zero in on the fine points. Don't dwell on the problems, accept Italy as a package deal. Savor your cappuccino, dangle your feet over a canal (if it smells, breathe with your mouth) and imagine what it was like a thousand years ago. Look into the famous sculpted eyes of Michelangelo's David, and understand Renaissance man's assertion of himself. Ramble through the rubble of Rome and mentally resurrect those ancient stones. Sit silently on a hilltop rooftop. Get chummy with the winds of the past. Write a poem over a glass of local wine in a sun-splashed, wave-dashed Riviera village. Get into it. Be a romantic. Italy is magic.

DAY 10
VENICE

Soak in this puddle of elegant decay all day long. Venice is Europe's best preserved big city. This car-free urban wonderland of more than one hundred islands, laced together by nearly five hundred bridges, born in a lagoon 1,500 years ago as a refuge from barbarians, is overloaded with tourists and slowly sinking (two unrelated facts). In the Middle Ages, after the Venetians smuggled in the bones of St. Mark (San Marco) and created a great trading empire, Venice became Europe's number one economic power. Venice has so much to offer and is worth at least a day on even the speediest tour. This itinerary gives it two nights and a day.

Suggested Schedule	
8:00 am	Breakfast.
8:30 am	Drop laundry off at laundromat, walk through town.
9:00 am	Basilica dei Frari and Scuola di San Rocco—for art lovers.
11:00 am	Accademia Gallery.
12:30 pm	Lunch.
2:00 pm	St. Mark's area—tour Doge's Palace, Basilica, ride to top of Campanile, glass blowing demonstration.
5:30 pm	Pick up laundry, siesta in hotel.
8:00 pm	Dinner or commence pub crawl.

Arriving in Venice
If you've never been there, Venice can be confusing. Actually, even if you have been there, it can be confusing. It's a car-less kaleidoscope of people, bridges and canals. It's like no other city. I wouldn't miss it.

Tourist information offices (located at Piazza Roma, where you'll park your car, at the train station and at St. Mark's Square) are open from 8:30 to 7:30. Confirm your sightseeing plans there—they have the latest hours listed.

Accept the fact that Venice was a tourist town 200 years ago, it's crowded today and it always will be. The crowds and tacky souvenir stalls vanish when you hit the back streets.

Transportation
By train you'll be dropped at the edge of town where you'll find a helpful tourist information office with maps and a room-find-

ing service. In front of the station you'll find the boat dock where the floating "city buses" *(vaporettos)* stop.

By car it's a bit trickier, as the freeway ends like Medusa's head. Follow the parking lot indicators. There are three or four locations with red or green lights indicating whether or not they have more room. Follow the signs to "Piazza Roma," the most convenient lot, and choose either the huge cheaper open lot or the safer, more expensive high-rise lot right on the square. From there you can visit the tourist information office and catch the boat of your choice deeper into Europe's most enchanting city.

Sightseeing Highlights—Venice

▲▲▲**Ride the Vaporettos**—Venice's floating city buses to anywhere in town for $1. Boat #1 is the slow boat down the Grand Canal (for the best do-it-yourself introductory tour). Number 5 offers a circular tour of the city (get off at Murano for glass-blowing). There are plenty of boats leaving from San Marco to the beach (Lido) as well as speedboat tours of Burano (a quiet, picturesque fishing and lace town), to Murano (glass-blowing island) and to Torcello (oldest churches and mosaics on an otherwise desolate island).

▲▲▲**Doge's Palace**—The former ruling palace has the second largest wooden room in Europe, virtually wallpapered by Tintoretto, Titian and other great painters. Nearby is the Bridge of Sighs and the prison (open 8:30-7, $3). No tours; buy guidebook in street.

▲▲**St. Mark's Basilica**—For 1,100 years it has housed the Saint's bones. Study the floor, treasures, the newly restored bronze horses upstairs, and views from the balcony. Modest dress (no shorts) usually required. (Open 10-5, free.)

▲▲**Campanile**—Ride the elevator ($1) up 300 feet for the best possible view of Venice. Notice photos on wall inside showing how this bell tower fell 80 years ago. Be on top when the bells ring for a most ear-shattering experience (ask about times). Open 9:30-8:30.

Bell Tower—See the bronze men (Moors) in action. Open 9-12 and 3-5, $2. Notice the world's first "digital" clock on the tower facing St. Mark's Square.

▲▲▲**Accademia**—Venice's greatest art museum is packed with the painted highlights of the Venetian Renaissance. Just over the wooden Accademia Bridge. Open 9-2, closed Mondays.

▲**Chiesa dei Frari**—A great church housing Donatello's wood-carving of St. John the Baptist, a Bellini, Titian's "Assumption" and much more. Open 9-Noon, 2:30-5:30.

▲**Scuola di San Rocco**—Next to the Frari church, another

lavish building bursting with art, including some 50 Tintorettos. Open 9-1, 3:30-6:30, last entrance a half hour before closing, $3.

Peggy Guggenheim Collection—A popular collection of far-out art that so many try so hard to understand. Includes works by Dali, Picasso and Pollock. Open Noon-6, closed Tuesdays $3; Sat 6-9 pm, free.

Evening: The stand-up-progressive-Venetian-pub-crawl-dinner

Venice's residential back streets hide plenty of characteristic bars with plenty of interesting toothpick munchie food. This is a great way to mingle and have fun with the Venetians. The best pubs are in the Castello district near the Arsenal and around the Campo Santa Maria di Formosa. Have a pizza on the square (at the pizzaria opposite the canal) and ask for Gigi's bar and Tony's bar, each one block away. Finish with gelato by the canal on the other side of Campo di Formosa. Italian hors d'oeuvres wait under glass in every bar. Try fried mozzarella cheese, blue cheese, calamari, artichoke hearts and the house wines. When you're good and ready, ask for a glass of *grappa*. Bars don't stay open very late so start your evening by 7:30 pm. Ask your hotel manager for advice—or to join you.

Nighttime is the right time in Venice. Soft summer nights, live music, floodlit history, a ceiling of stars, make St. Mark's magic at midnight. Howl at the moon. Dance with your shadow.

Helpful Hints

About wandering in Venice: Walk and walk, get as lost as possible. Notice how Venice is shaped like a fish. Explore the tail. Keep reminding yourself, "I'm on an island and I can't get off." When it comes time to find your way, look for arrows on walls at street corners to landmarks (San Marco, Rialto, etc.) or simply ask a local, *"Dove* (DOH' vay) *San Marco?"* (Where is St. Mark's?).

Traghetti: Where there are no bridges (and only three bridges cross the Grand Canal), gondolas ferry small loads of people across. These traghetti crossings are marked on any good map and cost only 200 lire (a dime). Considering that a touristic gondola ride costs about $40 for 45 minutes, these traghetti are a great deal.

Try a siesta in the Giardini Publici (public gardens, in the tail area), on the Isle of Burano, or in your hotel.

The best shopping area is around the Rialto Bridge and along the Merceria, the road connecting St. Mark's and the Rialto. Things are cheaper on the non-San Marco side of the Rialto bridge.

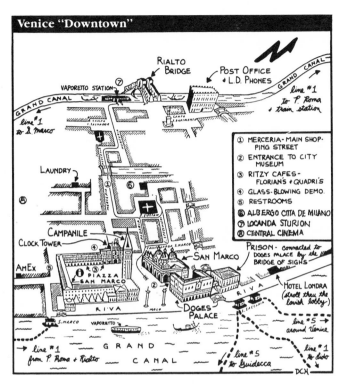

Venice "Downtown"

① MERCERIA - MAIN SHOP-
PING STREET
② ENTRANCE TO CITY
MUSEUM
③ RITZY CAFES -
FLORIAN'S + QUADRI'S
④ GLASS-BLOWING DEMO.
⑤ RESTROOMS
⑥ ALBERGO CITTA DE MILANO
⑦ LOCANDA STURION
⑧ CENTRAL CINEMA

If bombed by a pigeon, don't try to wipe it off immediately—
it'll just smear into your hair. Wait till it dries, then it will flake
off cleanly.

Food and Lodging
Venice is a notoriously difficult place to find a room. You can
minimize problems by (1) calling ahead to make a reservation,
(2) traveling off season, (3) arriving very early—as you will if
you take an overnight train ride from Munich, Vienna or Rome,
(4) staying in a mainland town nearby and sidetripping to
Venice, (5) using the tourist information office's room-finding
service. Calling ahead is the best approach.

I stay at the **Locanda Sturion** (S. Polo, Rialto, Calle Sturion
679, 30125 Venezia, tel. 5236243; from Austria or Germany dial
0039-41-5236243). Sergio or Sandro speak good English (normally in from 8 to 11 am) and will hold a room until 4:00 with
no deposit. Their hotel is 500 years old, located 100 yards from
the Rialto Bridge, opposite the boat dock, and doubles cost $30.

Another good bet is the **Albergo Citta di Milano** (Cam-

piello San Zulian, 590 San Marco, 30124 Venezia, tel. 27002),
wonderfully located near San Zulian church between the Rialto
and St. Mark's. The Venice youth hostel (on Giudecca Island,
Zittele stop on boat #5 or #8) is crowded, cheap and efficient.
Their budget cafeteria welcomes non-hostelers.

Three of my favorite restaurants are: 1) **Rosticceria San Bartolomeo** at Calle della Bissa 5424, near the Rialto Bridge, just
off Campo San Bartolomeo (busy, cheap, self-serve on ground
floor, great budget meals in full-serve restaurant upstairs). 2)
Trattoria de Remigio (Castello 3416, tel. 5230089, call in a
reservation; this popular place is wonderfully local and in a
great neighborhood for after-meal wandering). 3) **Trattoria
Douna Onesta** (3922 Dorsoduro, tel. 5229586) is a fun working class eatery serving cheap and good lunches and dinners
near the Ca Foscari. Also near the Ca Foscari is the University
Mensa (cafeteria). Tourists are welcome, fun atmosphere, $5
meals, 3rd floor above the fire department boats. For low stress
budget meals, you'll find plenty of self-service restaurants. One
is right at the Rialto Bridge.

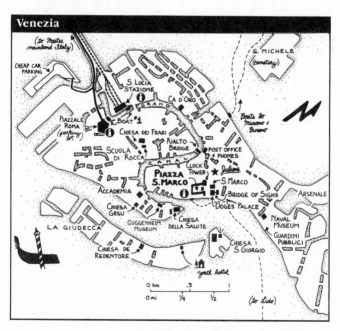

DAY 11
VENICE-FLORENCE-ROME

Today there are two goals: (1) travel from Venice to Rome, and (2) see Florence. Okay, of course you can't really see Florence in a day, but you can do pretty well. It's three hours by train or car from Venice to Florence and three more hours to Rome. If you leave early and arrive late you'll have seven or eight hours in Florence. So here's the plan: Leave Venice at the crack of dawn (don't wait for your hotel's skimpy breakfast). Even the pigeons will be sleepy as you march through the empty dawn streets. Have a hearty brunch en route. By 10:30 am you'll be in Europe's art capital and the heart of the Renaissance—Florence.

Suggested Schedule	
6:30 am	Leave Venice hotel without breakfast, catch canal boat.
7:15 am	Catch train or drive to Florence (breakfast en route).
11:00 am	David at Accademia.
11:45 am	Walk through old town, quick snack.
12:30 pm	Uffizi Gallery (best paintings).
2:00 pm	Shopping or Museo del Duomo for sculpture.
5:00 pm	Take train or drive south to Rome.
8:30 pm	Check into hotel (don't arrive in Rome late without a reservation).

Transportation
By car, traveling from Venezia (Venice) to Roma (Rome) via Firenze (Florence) is quite easy. It's autostrada (with reasonable tolls) all the way. From Venice, follow the signs to Bologna and then head for Firenze. Parking in Florence is horrendous at best. Follow the "centro" signs, park where you can and catch-a-cab to the Accademia. To leave, cross the St. Nicolo Bridge and follow the green signs south by autostrada to Roma.

At the edge of Rome, there's a freeway tourist office. If open, use their great room-finding service, confirm sightseeing plans and pick up a map while you're at it. Take the Via Salaria exit and work your way doggedly into the Roman thick of things. Avoid driving in Rome during rush hour. (You may find every hour is rush hour but some are even worse than others.) Parking in Rome is dangerous. Choose a well-lit busy street or a safe neighborhood. My favorite hotel is next to the Italian "Pentagon" —guarded by machine-gunners. In Rome, when all else

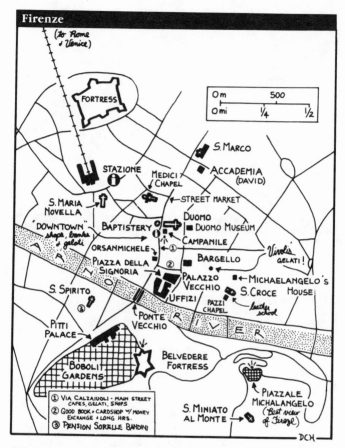

Firenze

(to Rome & Venice)

FORTRESS

0 m ____ 500
0 mi ____ 1/4 ____ 1/2

S. MARCO

STAZIONE
ACCADEMIA
(DAVID)

MEDICI CHAPEL

STREET MARKET

S. MARIA NOVELLA

Duomo
"DOWNTOWN"
shops, banks
& gelati
BAPTISTERY
Duomo Museum

ORSANMICHELE
CAMPANILE
Vivoli's GELATI!

PIAZZA DELLA SIGNORIA
BARGELLO

S. SPIRITO
PALAZZO VECCHIO
MICHAELANGELO'S HOUSE

UFFIZI
S. CROCE

PAZZI CHAPEL
leather school

PONTE VECCHIO

PITTI PALACE

BOBOLI GARDENS
BELVEDERE FORTRESS

PIAZZALE MICHALANGELO
(Best view of Firenze)

S. MINIATO AL MONTE

① VIA CALZAIUOLI - MAIN STREET
   CAFES, GELATI, SHOPS
② GOOD BOOK & CARDSHOP W/ MONEY
   EXCHANGE & LONG HRS.
③ PENSION SORELLE BANDINI

— DCH —

fails, hire a cab and follow him to your hotel.

By train things are much easier. The Venice-Florence-Rome trains are fast and frequent, zipping you straight into the centrally located station. Use train time to eat, study and plan.

Florence

Florence requires organization—especially for a blitz tour. Most important, remember that some attractions close early, while others are open all day. Everything is within walking distance of the station and the town center. Our suggested walk starts at the Accademia (home of Michelangelo's masterpiece, David), and cuts through the heart of the city to the Ponte Vecchio (old bridge) on the Arno River. See everyone's essential sight, David, right off. In Italy a masterpiece in the hand is worth two down the street; you never know when a place will unexpectedly lock up. Then walk down the street to the Cathedral, or Duomo. Check out the famous doors and the interior of the Baptistry. Farther down that street notice the statues on the exterior of the Or San Michele church and grab a quick lunch nearby. Around the corner are the central square (Piazza della Signoria), the city palace (Palazzo Vecchio) and the great Uffizi Gallery—all very important.

After you walk past the statues of the great men of the Renaissance in the Uffizi courtyard, you'll get to the Arno River and the Ponte Vecchio. Your introductory walk will be over, but your Florence experience will have just begun. After the overview, you'll still have half a day to see a lifetime of art and history—or just to shop, people-watch and enjoy Europe's greatest ice cream. Here are a few ideas:

Sightseeing Highlights
▲▲▲**The Accademia**—Houses Michelangelo's David and his powerful Prisoners. Eavesdrop as tour guides explain these masterpieces. There's also a lovely Botticelli painting. (Open Tues.-Sat. 9-2, Sun. 9-1, closed Monday, $3.) Be careful: most Italian museums allow the last visitors in 30 minutes before closing. There's a great book and poster shop across the street. The chubby 6,000-lire Florence book is my choice. Behind the Accademia is the Piazza della Annunziacione with its lovely Renaissance harmony, and the Hospital of the Innocents by Brunelleschi with terracotta medallions by della Robbia— often considered the first Renaissance building.

▲ **San Marco**—Near the Accademia, this museum houses the greatest collection anywhere of dreamy medieval frescos and paintings by the pre-Renaissance master, Fra Angelico. You'll see why he thought of his painting as a form of prayer and couldn't paint a crucifix without shedding tears. Also see Savonarola's monastic cell. Tues.-Sat. 9-2, Sun. 9-1, closed Monday.

▲▲**The Duomo**—The cathedral of Florence is a mediocre Gothic building capped by a magnificent Renaissance dome— the first Renaissance dome, by Brunelleschi, and the model for domes to follow. (When working on St. Peter's in Rome, Michelangelo said, "I can build a dome bigger but not more beautiful than the dome of Florence.") You can climb to the top but I'd recommend climbing Giotto's Tower next to it—faster, not so crowded and better view (including dome). Tower is open 8:30-12:30, 2:30-5:30.

▲▲**Museo del Duomo**—The Cathedral Museum, just behind the church at #9, has many Donatello statues and a Michelangelo Pieta. Great if you like sculpture. (Mon.-Sat. 9:30-1, 2:30-5:30,

Sun. 10-1.) This is one of the few museums in Florence open in the afternoon.

▲▲**The Baptistry**—Michelangelo said its gates were fit for paradise. Check out the famous carved bronze doors by Ghiberti—a breakthrough in perspective, using mathematical laws to create the illusion of 3-D on a 2-D surface (always open). Go inside for the medieval mosaic ceiling. Compare that to the "new improved" art of the Renaissance. 9:30-12:15, 2:30-5:15.

Or San Michele—Mirroring Florentine values, it was a combination church-grainery. Notice the spouts for grain to pour through the pillars inside. Also study the sculpture on its outside walls. You can see man literally stepping out in the great Renaissance sculptor Donatello's "St. George."

▲**Palazzo Vecchio**—The fortified palace of the Medici family. If you've read your history, this is exciting—otherwise skip it. Open 9-7.

▲▲▲**Uffizi Gallery**—The greatest collection of Italian painting anywhere. A must with plenty of works by Giotto, Leonardo, Raphael, Caravaggio, Rubens, Titian, Michelangelo and a roomful of Botticellis—a sight from which you may never recover. There are no tours, so buy a book on the street before entering. The museum is nowhere near as big as it is great. Few tourists spend more than two hours inside. The paintings are wonderfully displayed on one floor in chronological order. Good view of the Arno River. (Open 9-2; Sun. 9-1; closed Monday, $3.) Enjoy the Uffizi square full of artists, souvenir stalls and all the surrounding statues of the earth-shaking Florentines of 500 years ago.

▲▲**Bargello**—The city's greatest sculpture museum is just behind the palace (5 minutes walk from Uffizi). Donatello's David, Michelangelo works, much more. Very underrated. Open 9-2, Sun 9-1, closed Monday.

▲**Medici Chapel**—Incredibly lavish High Renaissance architecture and sculpture by Michelangelo. Open all day, surrounded by lively market scene.

▲ **Science Museum**—A fascinating collection of Renaissance and later clocks, telescopes, maps and ingenious gadgets. Also, you can see Galileo's finger in a little shrine-like bottle. English guidebooks are available. It's friendly, comfortably cool and never crowded. Just west of the Uffizi, entry near the river.

▲ **Michelangelo's Home**—Fans will enjoy his house on Via Ghibellina, #70.

▲ **The Pitti Palace**—Across the river, it has a giant art collection with works of the masters, plus more modern Italian art (lovely) and the huge landscaped Boboli Gardens—a cool refuge from the city heat.

▲**Piazzale Michelangelo**—Across the river (look for the statue of David), this square is worth the hike or the drive for the view. Just beyond it is the lovely little San Miniato church.

There's much, much more. Buy a guidebook. Doublecheck your plans with the tourist office. Remember, many museums call it a day at 2 pm and let no one in after 30 minutes before closing. Most are closed Monday, and at 1 pm on Sunday.

Best views of Florence are from Piazzale Michelangelo (30-minute uphill walk, across the river), from the top of the Duomo or Giotto's Tower, and in the poster and card shops.

Shopping

Florence is a great shopping town. Busy street scenes and markets abound (especially San Lorenzo, the Mercato Nuovo, on the bridge, and near Santa Croce). Leather, gold, silver, art prints and tacky "mini-Davids" are most popular. Check out the leather school of the Santa Croce church, inside on the right. Of course, gelato is a great Florentine edible art form . . . Italy's best ice cream is in Florence (especially at Vivoli's on Via Stinche—see map—at "Festival del Gelato," or at "Perche Non," both just off the pedestrian street running from the Duomo to the Uffizi). That's one souvenir that won't clutter your luggage.

Food and Lodging

Florence is one of Europe's most crowded, difficult and over-priced cities when it comes to finding a bed. The easiest plan is not to sleep here. If you do need a bed, call ahead or arrive early and take advantage of the tourist office near the station. I stay at **Pensione Sorelle Bandini** (in a 500-year-old palace on a scruffy square two blocks from the Pitti Palace just across the old bridge. Wonderful balcony lounge, English spoken, $30 doubles. Piazza Sancto Spirito #9, 50125 Firenze, tel. 055-215308) or at **Pensione Florentia** (just 100 yards behind the Duomo at #10 Piazza Brunelleschi, 50121 Firenze, tel. 055-213138).

While there are some special budget restaurants listed in most guidebooks, in Florence I keep it fast and simple, lunching in one of countless self-serve joints, Pizza Rusticas or just picnicking (juice, yogurt, cheese, roll: $2). For an interesting very cheap lunch drop by the **Casa di San Francesco** at Piazza SS. Annunziata 2 (monastery lunches, noon to 2:30, weekdays). Eat after 2:00 when the museums are closed.

Optional Itinerary

Taking in Venice, Florence, Rome—bing, bing, bing—is asking for sensory overload. Especially by train. It might be preferable to do Venice, take the night train to Rome, see the hill towns and go on to Florence. Or, you could make Florence a home base for some small-town exploring before you hit Rome, or more peacefully, make a small town (like Arezzo) your home base, and sidetrip into Florence as well as into the surrounding country-side before plunging into Rome. By seeing the hilltowns on your way south, you could night-train from Rome directly to the Italian Riviera (La Spezia), spend 14 hours on the beaches and in the villages and night-train again into Switzerland.

Also, if driving consider breaking the V-F-R crush by stop-ping at the hilltowns before Rome.

(A general mid-trip note: I assume I've already lost the readers who refuse to accept blitz travel as a realistic option for the over-worked American who can get two weeks off and "call in well" for a third if he's lucky, and who desperately wants to see the all-stars of European culture. So we'll unashamedly accept our time limitations and do our darndest—resting when we get home.)

DAYS 12 and 13
ROME

Rome is magnificent. Your ears will ring, your nose will turn your Kleenex black, you'll be run down or pick-pocketed if you're sloppy enough, and you'll be frustrated by chaos that only an Italian can understand. But you must see Rome. If your hotel provides a comfy refuge; if you pace yourself, accepting and even partaking in the siesta plan; if you're well-organized for sightseeing; and if you protect yourself and your goodies with extra caution and discretion, you'll do fine. You may see the sights and leave satisfied—you may even fall in love with the Eternal City.

Rome wasn't built in a day—nor can it be seen in a day—so let's take two. Focusing selectively on the highlights of Ancient Rome, Baroque Rome and the Vatican, two well-organized days can be very productive.

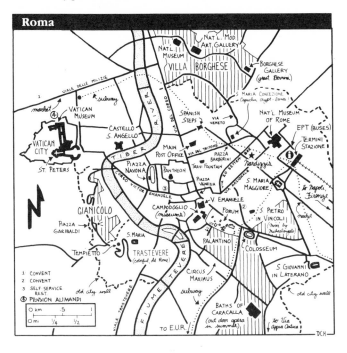

Suggested Schedule

Day 12

7:45 am	Breakfast.
8:30 am	St. Peter in Chains Church to see Michelangelo's Moses (admittedly out of historical sequence but it opens at 8 am and is a short walk from the Colosseum which opens at 9 am).
9:00 am	Colosseum.
10:00 am	Roman Forum.
11:30 am	Mammertine Prison, Capitoline Hill (Campidoglio) square by Michelangelo and museums (history and sculpture), Piazza Venezia, Victor Emmanuel Monument.
1:00 pm	Return to hotel, self-serve restaurant (ask receptionist for recommendation) and siesta.
3:00 pm	St. Peter's Cathedral—church, crypt, hike to top of dome (allow one hour), treasury, square, post office. Great free English tours at 3:15 from the portico.
6:30 pm	Explore Trastevere, outdoor dinner across the river in colorful Campo di Fiori restaurant.
9:00 pm	Walk home—Piazza Navona (tartufo ice cream at Tre Scalinis), Pantheon, Trevi Fountain (toss in two coins if you must), Spanish Steps (very overrated, best at night), and home by subway (last ride 11:30). Catch a taxi early if you run out of steam.

Day 13

8:00 am	Breakfast.
9:00 am	Pantheon.
10:00 am	Allow free time for additional sightseeing or shopping and lunch. Consider Gesu Church (headquarters of the Jesuits), Church of St. Ignatius (false dome), and Sta. Maria Sopra Minerva (only Gothic in Rome, Michelangelo statue), all near Pantheon.
1:30 pm	Vatican museum.
4:00 pm	Leave Rome for hill towns, two hours north.

Transportation

Day 1: Walk from St. Peter's in Chains to Piazza Venezia, take cab or bus to hotel. Then go by cab or bus back to the Vatican and to Trastevere (Santa Maria). Walk from Santa Maria in Trastevere to hotel or finish early with taxi.

Day 2: Use taxis or buses. Take subway from Vatican (Ottaviano stop) to train station (Terminal).

Sightseeing Highlights
▲**San Pietro in Vincoli (St. Peter in Chains) Church**—On exhibit are the original chains and Michelangelo's Moses. This is one of the few sights that opens before 9 am. Here and throughout Italy, use the recorded information boxes—just dial English and put in 200 lire. Also, in a place like this, it's worth using the coin-op lightning box. If you haven't already, buy the little $3 Rome book with map. 6:30-12:30, 3-7.

▲▲▲**Colosseum**—THE great example of Roman engineering, 2000 years old. Putting two theaters together, the Romans created an amphitheater capable of seating 50,000 people. Read up on it. Climb to the top. Subway stops here. Watch out for gypsy thief gangs—usually very young timid-looking girls. Check out the small red books with plastic overleafs to unruin the ruins. They're priced at 20,000 lire—pay only 10,000. Very helpful. Open 9-7.

▲▲▲ **Foro Romano (Roman Forum)**—The civic center of the city and its birthplace. The common ground of the seven hills. Climb the Palatine Hill (where the emperor's palaces were) for a great view, and mentally piece together the rubble of the Forum with the help of the artist's reconstruction in your $3 guidebook. For the studious, special Forum guidebooks are available. Open 9-6, closed Tuesday.

Mammertine Prison—The 2,500-year-old converted cistern which once imprisoned Saints Peter and Paul is worth a look. On the walls are lists of prisoners (Christian and non-Christian) and how they were executed (Strangolati, Morte de Fame, etc.). At the top of the stairs leading to the Campidoglio you'll find a cool water fountain. Use it. Block the spout with your fingers—it spurts up for drinking. You'll look quite Roman. Open 9-12:30, 2-6:30.

▲**Capitoline Hill (Campidoglio)**—The famous square designed by Michelangelo is three-sided (OK, it's not really a square), with two fine museums and the mayoral palace facing each other. The museum closest to the river is most important. Outside the entrance, notice the marriage announcements. You'll probably see a few blissfully attired newlyweds as well. Inside the courtyard have some photo fun with chunks of a giant statue of Emperor Constantine. (A w.c. is hidden around the corner.) The museum is worthwhile, with lavish rooms housing several great statues including the original (500 B.C.) Etruscan she-wolf and the enchanting Commodus as Hercules. Across the square is a museum full of ancient statues—great if you like portrait busts of forgotten emperors. Both open Tues.-

Sat. 9-2, Tues. and Thurs. 5-8, Sat. 8:30-11, Sun. 9-1. As you
walk down the grand stairway toward Piazza Venezia, notice the
cage on your right housing the city's mascot, the she-wolf.
From here, walk back up to approach the great square the way
Michelangelo wanted you to. At the bottom of the stairs, look
up the long stairway to your right for a good example of the
earliest style of Christian church—and be thankful you don't
need to climb these steps. Farther on, look into the ditch (on
the right) and see how everywhere modern Rome is built upon
the countless bricks and forgotten mosaics of ancient Rome.
Down the street on your left you'll see a modern building
actually built around surviving ancient pillars and arches.

Piazza Venezia—This square is the focal point of modern
Rome. The via del Corso, starting here, is the city's axis
(surrounded by the classiest shopping district). From the
balcony above the square, Mussolini whipped up the
nationalistic fervor of Italy, and the masses filled the square
screaming, "Right on! Il Duce!" (Fifteen years later they hung
him from a meathook in Milano.)

Victor Emmanuel Monument—Loved only by the ignorant
and his relatives, most Romans call this huge chunk of touristic
tofu in a cultural candy shop "the wedding cake," "the type-
writer" or "the dentures." It wouldn't be so bad if it weren't
sitting on a priceless chunk of Ancient Rome.

▲▲▲**Pantheon**—The greatest look at the splendor of Rome,
this best-preserved interior of antiquity is a must (open 9-2,
Sun 9-1, closed Monday). Sit inside and study it. Its dome, 140
feet high and wide, was Europe's largest until Brunelleschi's
dome was built in Florence 1,200 years later. In a little square to
the left, past the Bernini elephant and Egyptian obelisk statue, is
a small church with a little-known Michelangelo statue. Nearby
you'll find the church, Chiesa di St. Ignazio, with a fake fun (and
flat) cupola and the very rich and baroque Gesu Church, headquarters of the Jesuits.

▲▲**Piazza Navona**—Rome's most interesting night scene if
you like street music, artists, fire eaters, local Casanovas, great
ice cream (tartufo), outdoor cafes, hippies, and a fine Bernini
fountain (he's the father of Baroque art), in an oblong square
molded around a long-gone ancient chariot race track. Don't
joke around with the bulletproof-vested machine gunner you'll
pass as you walk toward the Pantheon. Best daytime view is
from the top floor of the City of Rome Museum.

Via del Corso—The city's youth stroll here from the Piazza
del Popolo down a wonderfully traffic-free section each evening around 6:00 . High fashion shops, antiques, people-watching. On Tuesdays, Thursdays and Saturdays, continue down to
the Victor Emmanuel Monument. Climb Michelangelo's

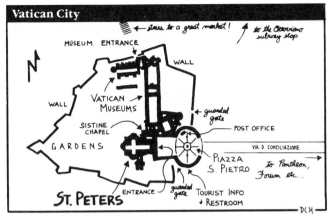

stairway to his glorious Campidoglio Square and visit the museum. Lovely view as the horizon reddens.

▲**Villa Borghese**—Rome's "Central Park" is great for people-watching (plenty of modern Romeos and Juliets). You can have a row in the lake and visit museums containing fantastic Baroque paintings, an Etruscan collection and modern art.

▲**National Museum of Rome**—Directly in front of the station, it houses the greatest ancient Roman sculpture.

▲**Trastevere**—The best look at old modern Rome is across the Tiber River. Colorful street scenes: pasta rollers, street-wise cats, crinkly old political posters encrusting graffiti-laden walls. There are motionless men in sleeveless T-shirts framed by open windows, cobbles with centuries of life ground into their cleavages, kids kicking soccer balls into the cars that litter their alley-fields. The action all marches to the chime of the church bells. Go there and wander. Wonder. Be a poet. This is Rome's "Left Bank."

▲▲**Ostia Antica**—Rome's ancient seaport (100,000 people in the time of Caesar, later a ghost town, now excavated) is the next best thing to Pompeii and, I think, Europe's most under-rated sight. Start at the 2,000-year-old theater, buy a map, explore the town, finishing with its fine little museum. Get there by subway from downtown. Just beyond is the beach (Lido)—interesting, but crowded and filthy.

The Vatican City—This tiny independent country is contained within Rome. Politically powerful, the Vatican is the religious capital of 800 million Roman Catholics. It deserves maximum respect regardless of your religious beliefs.

▲▲▲**St. Peter's Basilica**—There is no doubt: this is the biggest, richest and most impressive church on earth. To call it vast is an understatement; marks on the floor show where the

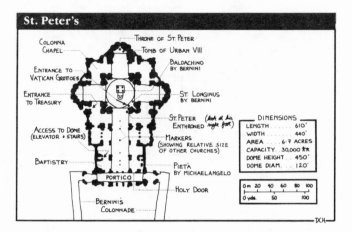

next largest churches would fit if they were put inside. The
ornamental cherubs would dwarf a large man. Birds roost
inside, and thousands of people wander about, heads craned
heavenward, hardly noticing each other. Don't miss Michelangelo's
Pieta to the right of the entrance. Bernini's altar work and huge
bronze canopy are brilliant (open 7-7 daily). The treasury and
the crypt are also important (open 9-12:30, 3-4:30). Wonderful
English guided tours (free, 90 minutes) normally leave at 3:15
from the portico. A guidebook is essential. Call the Vatican
Tourist Info to confirm sightseeing plans (tel. 6984466).

   The dome, Michelangelo's last work, is (of course) the biggest
anywhere. Taller than a football field is long, it is well worth the
climb (537 steps) for a great view of Rome, of the Vatican
grounds and of the inside of the Basilica (open 8-4:45 daily,
catch the elevator inside the church). Remember to dress
modestly—long pants or dress, shoulders covered.

▲▲▲**The Vatican Museum**—Too often treated as an obstacle
course separating the tourist from the Sistine Chapel, this is one
of Europe's top three or four houses of art. It can be exhausting,
so plan your visit carefully, focusing on a few themes, and allow
several hours. (Required: Sistine and Raphael rooms, Pio-
Clementine, Pinacoteca painting collection. Recommended:
Modern religious art, Egyptian, Etruscan.) The museum clearly
marks out four color-coded visits of different lengths. Rent the
headphones ($3) to get a recorded tour of the Raphael rooms
and Michelangelo's Sistine masterpiece. These rooms are the
pictorial culmination of the Renaissance. (Summer hours: 9-5,
Sat-Sun 9-2; off season: 9-2. Last entry an hour before closing.
Sistine and Raphael always open but many rooms close from
1:45 to 2:45 or from 1:30 on. $5.)

The museum book and card shop is great, offering, for example, a priceless ($6) black-and-white photo book of the Pieta, which I stock up on for gifts. The museum and the Piazza San Pietro have a Vatican post office with comfortable writing rooms. The Vatican post is the only reliable mail service in Italy (it must go via the Holy Spirit) and the stamps are a collectible bonus.

Capuchin Crypt—Below Santa Maria della Concezione on Via Veneto near Piazza Barberini. If you want bones, this is it. There are thousands of skeletons all artistically arranged for the delight or disgust of the always wide-eyed visitor. Do read the monastic message so you'll understand this as more than just an exercise in bony gore. Pick up a few of Rome's most interesting postcards. (Open 9-12, 3-6:30.)

E.U.R.—Mussolini's planned suburb of the future (50 years ago) is just a ten-minute subway ride from the Colosseum. Very impressive with a great history museum including a large scale model of ancient Rome. Fascist architecture at its repulsive best.

Overrated Sights—Spanish Steps (with the world's largest MacDonalds) and Trevi Fountain (but very central, free and easy to see, best at night). The Catacombs—no bones, way out of the city, commercialized.

Helpful Hints

Place to meet a rich and sexy single Italian (or just look): the street-side cafes of Via Veneto.

For Tired Tourists: taxis are not expensive if the meter is turned on. The subway system (Metropolitana) is simple, cheap and fast. Bus routes are charted on most maps and clearly listed at the stops. Buy tickets at Tobac shops and learn why the system is named ATAC. Save time and legwork whenever possible by telephoning. When the feet are about to give out, sing determinedly, "Roman, Roman, Roman, keep those doggies movin'. . . ."

In museums, "A.C." (Avanti Christo, or "Before Christ") after a year is the same as our B.C. "D.C." (Dopo Christo) is what we call A.D. Shops and offices are open 9 am-1 pm, 4 pm-8 pm; museums, 9 am-2 pm, closed on Mondays and at 1 pm on Sundays. Outdoor sights like the Colosseum, Forum and Ostia Antica, are open 9 am-7 pm, often closed one day a week. The Capitoline Hill museums are Rome's only nocturnal museums, open Tuesdays and Thursdays, 5 pm-8 pm and Saturday 8:30 pm-11 pm, churches open very early and close for lunch. Dress modestly—no bare shoulders or shorts.

There are no absolutes in Italy and these hours may vary inexplicably. In the holiday month of August, many shops and restaurants close up— *"Chiuso per fereria"* signs decorate locked doors all over town. "Closed for restoration" is another sign you'll see all too often, especially in the winter.

If you stay at Pension Nardizzi, ask for a city map. It's free, listing sights, hours and bus lines.

Food and Lodging
Rome is difficult only because of its overwhelming size. There are plenty of rather tatty *pensioni* for budget ($10 per person) beds. Via Palestro is lined with cheap pensions. In Rome I often get a nicer place—spending more money—for its peaceful oasis/refuge value. The convents of the city are your most interesting budget bet. They operate tax-free, so are cheaper. These are obviously peaceful, safe and clean, but sometimes stern and usually "no speak English." Try the **Suore di Sant Anna** (Piazza Madonna dei Monti #3, 00184 Roma, tel. 06-485778). Three blocks from the Forum near via Serpentine, this is a place for Ukrainian pilgrims—not a privileged class in the USSR—and therefore they rarely visit, and these lodgings are usually empty. The sisters speak Italian, Portuguese and, of course, Ukrainian—good luck. If you land a spot, it's great atmosphere and heavenly meals, with unbeatable location and price.

Near the Vatican Museum on #42 via Andrea Doria is the **Suore** (convent) **Oblate Dell Assunzione** (tel. 3599540, $6 per night, no meals). Spanish, French and Italian spoken in a fun neighborhood across from a colorful market. Just across the street from the Vatican Museum is the Convent at Viale Vaticano #92 (tel. 350209). They take men and women but no reservations, and are normally full but worth a try. My choices for more normal accommodations are **Pension Alimandi** (friendly, speaks English, $25 doubles, one block in front of the Vatican Museum, Via Tunisi 8, 00192 Roma, tel. 06/6799343) and **Pension Nardizzi** (via Firenze #38, 00184 Roma, tel. 06/460368, in a safe, handy and central location, 5-minute walk from central station and Piazza Barberini on the corner of Via Firenze and Via XX Septembre.) Pension Nardizzi is expensive ($45 per double with breakfast) but worth the splurge if you've got the urge. Sr. Nardizzi speaks English.

Otherwise the area around the station seethes with accommodations of all styles. Do arrive early or call ahead if possible. The central station (Termini) is a jack of all trades with a bank that's open late, tourist information, room-finding service, a day hotel, subway station and major city bus station. Pick up the periodical entertainment guide, "Qui Roma" (Here's Rome).

Hotels can recommend the best nearby cafeteria or restaurant. A handy self-serve is **Il Delfino**, corner of Via Argentina and

Via Vittorio Emmanuel near the Pantheon. Also near the Pantheon
(two blocks in front down Via Maddalena, around the corner to
the left) is **Hostaria la Nuova Capannina**, on Piazza della
Coppelle #8, close to Pantheon, with good, budget sit-down
meals. If your convent serves food, eat it. Avoid restaurants on
any famous square. In Trastevere I enjoyed **Il Comparone** on
Piazza in Piscinula #47, tel. 5816249. Near the Piazza Navona try
the restaurants on Campo Fiori for good food and great
atmosphere. **Piccadilly's** on Piazza Barberini is a good value
and the nearby **Ristorante Il Giardino** (Via Zucchelli 29, tel
465202, closed Mondays) is my favorite spot for a splurge. Near
the Vatican Museum and Pension Alimandi try **Restorante dei
Musei** (corner of Via Sebastiano Veneiro and Via Santamaura)
or the wonderful Via Andrea Doria marketplace at the bottom
of the steps (closed by 1:00).

The Great Escape
OK, the 22-day plan is to head for the hilltowns to end Day
Number 13. Drive one hour north to Orvieto, then leave the
freeway and under the evening sun, wind through fields and
farms to Bagnoregio, where the locals will direct you to
Angelino Catarcia's **Al Boschetto**, the only hotel in town ($25
per double, bed and breakfast). Angelino doesn't speak English;
he doesn't need to. Have an English-speaking Italian call him for
you from Rome, (tel. 0761-92369. Address: Strada Monterado,
Bagnoregio, Viterbo, Italy). His family is wonderful and if you
so desire, he'll get the boys together and take you deep into the
gooey, fragrant bowels of "The Cantina." Music and vino kills
the language barrier in Angelino's wine cellar. Angelino will
teach you his theme song, "Trinka, Trinka, Trinka." The lyrics
are easy (see previous sentence). Warning: descend at your own
risk—there are no rules unless the female participants set them.
If you are lucky enough to eat dinner at Angelino's ("bunny" is
the house specialty), ask to try the *dolce* (sweet) dessert wine.
Everything at Angelino's is deliciously homegrown—figs, fruit,
wine, rabbit, pasta.

When you leave the tourist crush, life as a traveler in Italy
becomes very easy. You should have no trouble finding rooms
in the small towns of Italy. You won't even need a list or
recommendations.

DAY 14
ITALIAN HILLTOWNS

Today is devoted to rural and small-town Italy—more
specifically, to the province of Umbria which, along with
Tuscany is noted for its enchanting time-passed towns and
villages. Driving from Bagnoregio towards Orvieto, we'll stop
just past Purano to tour an Etruscan tomb. Follow the yellow
road signs, reading Tomba Etrusca, to Giovanni's farm (a sight in
itself). Find the farmer and he'll take you out back and down
into the lantern-lit 2,500-year-old tomb discovered 100 years
ago by his grandfather. His Italian explanation is fun. Tip him a
dollar or two and drive on to Orvieto.

Orvieto, Umbria's grand hilltown, is no secret but well
worthwhile. Study its colorful Italian Gothic cathedral with
exciting Signorelli frescos. Across the street are a fine Etruscan
museum, a helpful tourist office, a great gelati shop and unusually
clean public toilets. Orvieto is famous for its ceramics and its
wine.

Drive back, stopping at Lubriano for a great view of Civita.
Follow the yellow signs through Bagnoregio to Civita. Park at
the end of town and walk the steep donkey path to the traffic-
free, 2,500-year-old, vast, canyon-swamped pinnacle town of
Civita di Bagnoregio. This town is magic, handle it carefully!
Al Forno (green door on main square) is the only restaurant in
town, and it's great for lunch. Ask for Anna there for a tour of
the little church (tip her and buy your post cards from her). A

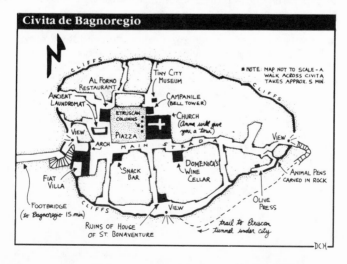

Civita de Bagnoregio

cute little museum (ask for "moo-ZAY'oh") is just around the
corner. Around the other corner is a cool and friendly wine
cellar, where Domenica serves local wine on a dirt floor with
stump chairs . . . 30 cents a glass. Civita offers lots more;
it's an Easter egg hunt and you're the kid.

Suggested Schedule	
8:30 am	Breakfast.
9:00 am	Drive to Etruscan tomb and tour it.
10:30 am	Orvieto.
1:00 pm	Free time in Civita di Bagnoregio.
Evening	Further exploration by car, or rest in hotel. Be sure you aren't missing any nearby fiestas.

Optional Itinerary
If you are traveling by train, touring the hilltowns will be much
more difficult. Italy's small-town public transportation is
miserable. You can take the one-hour bus trip from Orvieto (the
nearest train station) to Bagnoregio for $1 (3 buses run a day) or
hitchhike. From Bagnoregio walk out of town past the gate, turn
left at the pyramid monument and right at the first fork to get to
the hotel. Without your own wheels it might make sense to use
Orvieto as a home base. It's a good transportation hub. The

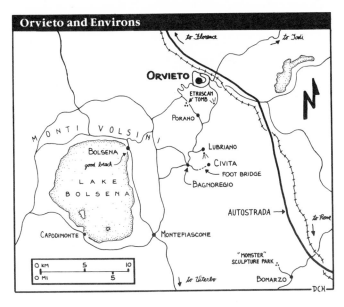

Orvieto and Environs

tourist office runs several good back-door-style day trips to
nearby towns.

For a fun and refreshing side trip take a dip in Lake Bolsena
nestled below an extinct volcano, 30 minutes by car from
Bagnoregio. **Ristorante Il Faro**, below the town of Montefiascone,
offers great meals on a leafy terrace overlooking the lake. Good
swimming! Nearby in Bomarzo is a monster park—possibly
Italy's tackiest sight.

Tuscany, the province just to the north, also has some
exciting hilltowns, many of which are served by trains and
more frequent buses. Whatever you do, rip yourself out of the
Venice-Florence-Rome syndrome. There's so much more to
Italy. Give yourself a few days in Tuscany and Umbria. Seek out
and savor its uncharted hilltowns. For starters, here's a map
listing a few of my favorites.

Tuscany & Umbria

DAY 15
NORTH TO PISA AND THE ITALIAN RIVIERA

With breakfast and plenty of cappuccino under your belt, hit the autostrada and drive north for about four hours, turning left at Florence, stopping at Pisa for lunch.

Pisa, a 30-minute drive out of the way, can be seen in about an hour. Its three important sights float regally on a lush lawn—the best grass in Italy, and ideal for a picnic. The Piazza of Miracles is the home of the famous Leaning Tower. The climb to the top is fun (294 tilted steps, open 8 am-7:30 pm). The huge cathedral (open 7:45 am-12:45 pm, 3 pm-6:45 pm) is actually more important artistically than the more famous tipsy tower. Finally, the Baptistry (same hours as church) is interesting for its great acoustics. The doorman uses its echo-power to actually sing haunting harmonies with himself. (Pisa has plenty of hotels, and you could make it your home base for a side trip into the Cinqueterre by direct train.)

One hour away is the port of La Spezia, where you'll park your car (hopefully at the station; otherwise, find a safe spot) and catch the 50-cent, 20-minute train ride into the Cinqueterre, Italy's Riviera wonderland.

Vernazza, one of five towns in the region, is the ideal home base, where, if you have called in advance, Sr. Sorriso will have dinner waiting. In the evening, wander down the main street (also the only street) to the harbor to join the visiting Italians in a sing-a-long. Have a gelato, cappuccino or glass of the local Cinqueterre wine at a waterfront cafe or on the bar's patio that overlooks the breakwater (follow the rope railing above the "soccer field," notice the photo of rough seas just above the door inside). Stay up as late as you like because tomorrow you can have a leisurely day.

Suggested Schedule	
8:00 am	Drive from Bagnoregio to Pisa.
12:00 pm	Picnic lunch, sightsee, Pisa.
2:00 pm	Drive to La Spezia.
3:30 pm	Train to Vernazza.
Evening	Free time in Vernazza.

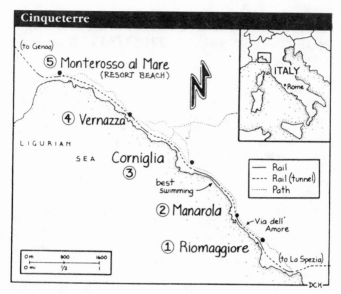

Cinqueterre Train Schedule
Trains leaving La Spezia for villages: 1:15, 4:02, 4:50, 5:36, 6:42,
7:15, 7:40, 9:05, 10:35, 11:39, 12:22, 13:23, 14:33, 15:32, 17:06,
17:52, 18:10, 19:08, 19:45, 20:49, 22:45, 23:40.
Trains leaving Vernazza for La Spezia: 0:32, 1:31, 4:42, 5:13,
6:08, 6:58, 7:17, 8:40, 9:46, 10:55, 12:17, 13:30, 14:37, 15:46,
16:50, 17:33, 18:42, 19:05, 19:37, 21:03, 21:47, 22:42, 23:10.

All trains stop at each Cinqueterre town. On the map, towns
#1, 2 & 3 are just a few minutes before or after Vernazza, town
#4. These trains are in the "Locale" class (Italian for "milk run").
Trains often run late.

Food and Lodging
While the Cinqueterre is unknown to the international mobs
that ravage the Spanish and French coasts, plenty of Italians
come here, so getting a room can be tough. August and weekends are bad. On weekends in August, forget it! But the area is
worth planning ahead for.

In Vernazza, my favorite town, stay at **Pension Sorriso** (the
only one in town), up the street from the station ($24 per per-
son includes bed, breakfast, dinner, a Mediterraean-style toilet
in the bar and the catchiest video game tune you'll ever have no
choice but to like, 19018 Vernazza, 5 Terre, La Spezia, tel.
0187-812224, English spoken). If that's full or too expensive, Sr.
Sorriso will help you find a private room. You can sleep free on

the trail to Monterosso or on the breakwater (check your bags at the station for 50 cents; showers on the beach; in the summer you won't be alone.)

In Riomaggiore, **Hotel Argentina** is above the town on Via di Gasperi #37. (tel. 0187-920213, $20 doubles, $28 triples). The restaurant in the center of town can usually find you a bed for $8.

In Manarola, **Marina Piccola** is located right on the water (tel. 0187-920103, around $15 per person).

When all else fails, you can stay in a noisy bigger town like La Spezia and take side trips into the villages.

Sorriso requires you take dinner from his pension; it's a forced luxury, and there is often fresh seafood. His house wine is great and, if you have an excuse to really celebrate, splurge on his strong, subtly sweet and unforgettable Sciachetre wine.

Elsewhere, in Vernazza, the **Castello** (castle) restaurant serves great food just under the castle with Vernazza twinkling below you and friendly Lorenzo at your service. The town's only gelati shop is excellent and most harborside bars will let you take your glass on a breakwater stroll.

This chart shows hiking time between the five villages of the Cinqueterre, as numbered on the map opposite. (Thinking of towns as numbers simplifies your beach life.)

DAY 16

VACATION FROM YOUR VACATION: THE ITALIAN RIVIERA

Take a free day to enjoy the villages, swimming, hiking, sun-shine, wine and evening romance of one of God's great gifts to tourism. Pay attention to the schedules, and take advantage of the trains.

Helpful Hints

Pack your beach and swim gear, wear your walking shoes and catch the train to Riomaggiore. Walk the cliff-hanging Via dell' Amore to Manarola and buy food for a picnic and hike to Cor-niglia for the best beach around. There's a shower there, a bar, and a cafe which serves light food. The swimming is great and there's a train to zip you home later on. Or hike back to Vernaz-za where you can enjoy the sweet sounds of the village's asylum for crazed roosters who cock-a-doodle at any hour—except dawn.

If you're into *la dolce far niente* and don't want to hike, you could take the train directly to Corniglia to maximize beach time.

If you're a hiker, hike from Riomaggiore all the way to Monterosso al Mare, where a sandy "front door" style beach awaits. Pick a cactus fruit and ask a local to teach you how to peel it, Delicioso!

Each beach has showers that probably work better than your hotel's. Bring soap and shampoo. This is a good sunny time to wash clothes. When you get to Switzerland, your laundry won't dry as fast.

On your last night in Italy, be romantic. Sit on the breakwater, wine in hand, music in the background and let the warm waves lap at your feet.

Optional Itinerary

Hurried train travelers (who did the hilltowns on their way south) can take the train overnight to La Spezia from Rome, check their bags there, have 14 hours of fun in the Cinqueterre sun (hike from Riomaggiore to Monterosso in the cool morning hours, mid-day on the beaches of towns 5 and 3, dinner and evening in Vernazza), and travel overnight again up to Switzer-land. This would overcome the tricky hotel situation altogether. I haven't found anything nearly as nice as the Cinqueterre in this area so day tripping from this region makes no sense at all.

DAY 17

THE ITALIAN RIVIERA TO THE ALPS

This is a long drive: scenic along the Mediterranean coast, boring during the stretch to Switzerland, and thrilling through the Alps.

Suggested Schedule	
7:00 am	Catch train.
7:30 am	Drive freeway north to Switzerland.
12:30 pm	Lunch in Bellinzona or nearby town.
1:30 pm	Drive to Sustenpass, take a break.
3:40 pm	Drive to Interlaken, 1-hour stop, drive on to Stechelberg.
6:45 pm	Catch 18:55 gondola to Gimmelwald.
7:00 pm	Learn why they say "If heaven isn't what it's cracked up to be, send me back to Gimmelwald."

Transportation
Catch the 7 am train (skip Sorriso's breakfast; you'll hurt no one's feelings). If your car's where you left it, drive it on the autostrada along the stunning Riviera, skirting Christopher Columbus' home town of Genoa, noticing the crowded highrise living conditions of the Italy that most tourists choose to avoid, turning north through Italy's industrial heartland, past Milano with its hazy black halo and on into Switzerland. This is Amaretto country; very cheap at any truck stop. Just over the border is the Italian-speaking Swiss Riviera with famous resorts like Lugano and Locarno.

Bellinzona is a good town for a lunch break (great picnic rest stop a few miles south of Bellinzona off the freeway) before climbing to the Alps. After driving through the Italian-speaking Swiss *canton* (state) of Ticino, famous for its ability to build just about anything out of stone, you'll take the longest tunnel in the world—the ten-mile-long Gotthard Pass Tunnel. It's so boring it's exciting. It hypnotizes most passengers into an open-jawed slumber until they pop out into the bright and cheery, green and rugged German-speaking Alpine world.

At Wassen (a good place to change money and, according to railroad buffs, the best place in Europe for train-watching) turn onto the Sustenpass road. Higher and higher you'll wind until you're at the snow-bound summit—a good place for a coffee or hot chocolate stop. Give your intended hotel a call, toss a few snowballs, pop in your "Sound of Music" cassette and roll on.

Descend into the Bernese Oberland, rounding idyllic Lake Brienz to Interlaken. Stop for an hour there (park at the West Station) to take care of some administrative business. Banks abound. The one in the station is fair and stays open Monday through Saturday until 7 pm. A great tourist information office is just past the handy post office on the main street. Interlaken is the high class resort of the region, with the best shopping.

From Interlaken drive 30 minutes south into Lauterbrunnen Valley, a glacier-cut cradle of Swiss-ness. Park at the head of the valley in the Stechelberg gondola lot (safe and free). Ride the huge cable car straight up for five minutes ($3) to traffic-free Gimmelwald village. A steep 100-yard climb uphill brings you to the chalet marked simply "Hotel." This is Walter Mittler's Hotel Mittaghorn; you have arrived.

Food and Lodging

While Switzerland bustles, Gimmelwald sleeps. It has a youth hostel, a pension, and a hotel. The hostel is simple, less than clean, rowdy, cheap ($3) and very friendly. It is often full, so call ahead to Lena, the elderly woman who runs the place (tel. 036-551704). The hostel has a self-serve kitchen and is one block from the lift station. This relaxed hostel is struggling to survive. Please respect its rules, leave it cleaner than you found it, and treat it with loving care. Next door is the pension with rooms and meals. Up the hill is the treasure of Gimmelwald: Walter Mittler, the perfect Swiss gentleman, runs a chalet called **Hotel Mittaghorn**. It's a classic Alpine-style place with a million-dollar view of the Jungfrau Alps. Walter is careful not to get too hectic or big and enjoys sensitive, back-door travelers. He runs the hotel alone, keeping it simple, but with class. . . He charges about $14 for bed and breakfast. (Address: 3826 Gimmelwald, Bern, Switzerland tel. 036-551658, English spoken.)

Other good budget beds are at **Masenlager Stocki** (Lauterbrunnen, tel. 551754), **Naturfreundehaus Alpenhof** (Stechelberg, 551202) and the **Chalet Schweizerheim Garni** ($20 per person in July and August, $15 off season, Wengen, 551581). Younger travelers love the cheap and yankee-oriented **Balmer's Herberge** in Interlaken (Hauptstr 23, in Matten, tel. 036-221961). Nearby towns have plenty of budget accommodations. Let each village's tourist office help you out.

Switzerland

- 16,000 square miles (one-fourth the size of Washington State).
- 6½ million people (400 per square mile, declining slightly).
- Switzerland, Europe's richest, best-organized and most

mountainous country, is an easy oasis and a breath of fresh Alpine air—much needed after intense Italy.

■ Switzerland, 60 percent of which is rugged Alps, has distinct cultural regions and customs. Two thirds of the people speak German, 20 percent French, 10 percent Italian, and a small group of people in the southeast speak Romansh, a direct descendant of ancient Latin. Within these four language groups, there are many dialects. An interest in these regional distinctions will win the hearts of locals you meet. As you travel from one valley to the next, notice changes in architecture and customs (the green Michelin guide is very helpful).

■ Historically, Switzerland is one of the oldest democracies. Born when three states, or cantons, united in 1291, the Confederation Helvetica as it's called (Roman name for the Swiss—notice "CH" on cars) grew, as our original 13 colonies did, to the 23 of today. The government is very decentralized and the canton is first on the Swiss citizen's list of loyalties.

■ Switzerland loves its neutrality, stayed out of both world wars, but is far from lax defensively. Every fit man serves in the army and stays in the reserve. Each house has a gun and a bomb shelter. Airstrips hide inside mountains behind Batmobile doors. With the push of a button, all road, rail and bridge entrances to the country can be destroyed, changing Switzerland into a formidable mountain fortress. The U.S.S.R. views Switzerland as a sort of "Capitalist Alamo" and considers its "armed neutrality" charming nonsense. August 1 is the very festive Swiss national holiday.

■ Switzerland has a low inflation rate and a very strong franc. Accommodations, gas and groceries are reasonable, and hiking is free, but alpine lifts and souvenirs are expensive. Shops throughout the land thrill tourists with carved, woven and clanging mountain knick-knacks, clocks, watches, and Swiss army knives. (Remember, Victorinox is the best brand.)

■ The Swiss eat when we do and enjoy rather straightforward, no-nonsense cuisine, delicious fondue, raclette, rich chocolates, fresh dairy products (try Muesli yogurt) and Fendant, a surprisingly good local white wine. The Co-op and Migros grocery stores are the hungry hiker's best budget bet.

■ You can get anywhere quickly on Switzerland's fine road system (the world's most expensive to build per mile), or on its scenic and efficient trains. Tourist information offices abound. While Switzerland's booming big cities are quite cosmopolitan, the traditional culture lives on in the Alpine villages. Spend most of your time getting high in the Alps. On Sundays you're most likely to enjoy traditional sports, music, clothing and culture.

DAY 18
ALP HIKE DAY

If the weather is decent, set today aside for hiking. The best hike is from Mannlichen to Kleine Scheidegg to Wengen. Get an early start, when the lifts are cheaper and the weather is usually better. Weather can change rapidly so always carry a sweater and raingear. Wear good walking shoes.

Recommended plan: Leave early. Ride lift to Murren, train to Grutschalp, funicular to Lauterbrunnen, cross the street and catch the train to Wengen. Do any necessary banking or picnic shopping. Catch cable car to Mannlichen. Hike to little peak for grand view, then walk (one hour) around to Kleine Scheidegg for lunch. There are a few restaurants or you can picnic. (To check the weather before investing in a ticket, call 551022.)

If you've got an extra $40 and the weather is perfect ride the train through the Eiger to the towering Jungfrajoch and back. From Kleine Scheidegg, enjoy the ever-changing Alpine panorama of the North Face of the Eiger, Jungfrau and Monch, probably accompanied by the valley-filling mellow sound of alp horns, as you hike gradually downhill (2 hours) to the town of Wengen. If the weather turns bad or you run out of steam, you can catch the train earlier. The trail is very good and the hike is easy for any fit person.

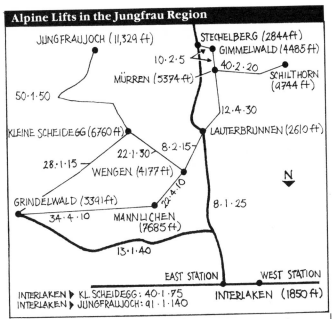

Alpine Lifts in the Jungfrau Region

JUNGFRAUJOCH (11,329 ft)

STECHELBERG (2844 ft)
GIMMELWALD (4485 ft)

10·2·5

40·2·20

MÜRREN (5374 ft)

SCHILTHORN (9744 ft)

50·1·50

12·4·30

KLEINE SCHEIDEGG (6760 ft)

LAUTERBRUNNEN (2610 ft)

8·2·15

22·1·30

28·1·15

WENGEN (4177 ft)

12·4·10

N

GRINDELWALD (3391 ft)

8·1·25

34·4·10

MANNLICHEN (7685 ft)

13·1·40

EAST STATION   WEST STATION

INTERLAKEN ▶ KL. SCHEIDEGG: 40·1·75   INTERLAKEN (1850 ft)
INTERLAKEN ▶ JUNGFRAUJOCH: 91·1·140

Code: Roundtrip price in Swiss francs—Departures per hour—
Length of ride in minutes (e.g., 13·1·40 is 13 SF roundtrip,
1 per hour, 40 minutes long).

Round trips are discounted only above towns (i.e., to Kl.
Scheidegg & Schilthorn). Buy one-way between towns for
flexibility. Maps, schedules and price lists are available at any
station. Lifts run from about 7 am to 8 pm. Groups of five or
more receive about a 20% discount. Discount Jungfraujoch
trains leave Kl. Scheidegg at 8:07, 9:07, 15:03, 16:00 and 17:10.
Other rides cost 16 SF more than price above. Stechelberg to
Gimmelwald: 25 & 55 past the hour, until 19:25.

Wengen is a fine shopping town. Avoid the steep and boring
final descent by catching the train from Wengen to Lauterbrunnen. Ride back up to Grutschalp, take the scenic train or hike to
Murren, and walk back down to Hotel Mittaghorn (45 minutes).
Total cost of today's lifts—around $20.

Evening fun in Gimmelwald is found in the hostel (lots of
young Alp-happy hikers and a good chance to share information on the surrounding mountains) and up at Walter's. If you're
staying at Walter's, don't miss his dinner, Then sit on his porch
and watch the sun lick the mountain tops to bed as the moon
rises over the Jungfrau.

DAY 19

FREE TIME IN THE ALPS, EVENING DRIVE INTO FRANCE

If the weather's good, take another hike. The Schilthorn offers the most Alpine excitement around. Late in the afternoon it's time to move on, driving out of the Alps and into France's Alsace region to Colmar—a whole new world.

Suggested Schedule	
7:30	Catch gondola to Schilthorn.
8:00	Breakfast at 10,000 feet.
9:00	Free in Alps to hike or shop in Murren.
12:00	Picnic in Murren or back at Walter's.
1:00	Gondola to Stechelberg, drive to Bern.
2:00	Explore downtown Bern.
4:00	Drive to Colmar.

Transportation

If you're driving, by 4 pm you should be speeding out of the mountains, past the Swiss capital of Bern and on towards Basel, where Switzerland snuggles against both Germany and France.

Before Basel you'll go through a tunnel and come to Reststatte Pratteln Nord, a strange orange structure that looks like a huge submarine laying eggs on the freeway. Stop here for dinner and a look around one of Europe's greatest freeway stops. There's a bakery and grocery store for picnickers, a restaurant and a bank open daily until late. Spend some time goofing around, then carry on (Interlaken to Colmar is a 4-hour drive). From Basel follow the signs to France. In France head north to Colmar, where you can park on the huge square called Place Rapp, and check into the nearby Hotel Le Rapp. Wander around the old town, have a dessert crepe, or some local wine.

For train travelers, the Eurailpass won't work on the mountain lines south of Interlaken. Upon arrival in Interlaken ask about the Jungfrau Region trains—schedules, prices and special deals. Also, lay the groundwork for your departure by getting the Interlaken-Colmar schedule. It's a very easy trip. From the Colmar station you can walk to Hotel Le Rapp, about 10 minutes.

Helpful Hints

Walter serves a great breakfast, but if the weather's good, skip his and eat on top of the Schilthorn, at 10,000 feet, in a slowly

France

revolving mountain-capping restaurant (of James Bond movie
fame). The early-bird special gondola tickets (rides before 9:00
a.m.) take you from Gimmelwald to the Schilthorn and back
with a great continental breakfast on top for about $25. (Get
tickets at the Station or from Walter.). Try the Birchermuesli-
yogurt treat. Walter has special discount tickets which include a
hearty Continental breakfast on top.

For hikers: The gondola (Gimmelwald-Schilthorn-Gimmelwald)
ride costs about $28. The hike (G-S-G) is free, if you don't mind
a 5,000-foot altitude gain. I ride up and hike down or, for a less
scary hike, go up and half way down by cable car and walk
down from the Birg station. Lifts go twice an hour and the ride
takes 30 minutes. (The round-trip excursion early-bird fare is
cheaper than Gimmelwald-Schilthorn-Birg. If you buy the
ticket you can decide at Birg if you want to hike or ride down.)
Linger on top. Watch hang gliders set up, psych up and take off,
flying 30 or 40 minutes with the birds to distant Interlaken.
Walk along the ridge out back. You can even convince yourself
you climbed to that perch and feel pretty rugged. Think twice
before descending from the Schilthorn (weather can change,
have good shoes). Most people would have more fun hiking

down from Birg. Just below Birg is a mountain hut. Drop in for
soup, cocoa, or a coffee-schnapps. You can spend the night for
$5 (tel. 036/552640).

The most interesting trail from Murren to Gimmelwald is the
high one via Gimmlin. Murren has plenty of shops, bakeries,
tourist information, banks, a modern sports complex...

Food and Lodging
In general, France is wonderful for the budget traveler. Any
one-star or two-star hotel (indicated by a blue-and-white plaque
near the door) will offer bed and breakfast for around $10 per
person. Popular Colmar and Alsace can be difficult in peak
season so, as usual, it's wise to arrive early or call ahead. **Hotel
Le Rapp** in Colmar is ideal (Rue Berthe-Molly, tel. 03389-416210
from another country or 89-416210 from France). Friendly, intimate, with a great local restaurant, $15 doubles, English
spoken. It's run by Bernard, who mixes class with warmth like
no man I've met. If he's full, ask him for a recommendation.
Hotel Turenne (10 Rt. de Bale, tel. 89-411226) and **La
Chaumiere** (74 Ave de la Republique, tel. 410899) are also
good. The tourist information office can also find you a room.
Nearby towns and villages aren't so crowded and can offer an

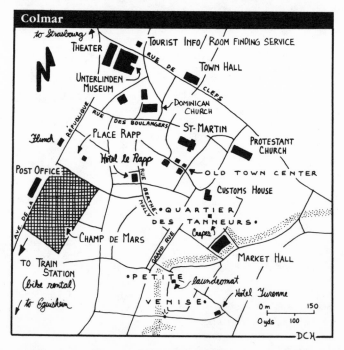

even more Alsacian hotel experience. But Colmar is your best headquarters town.

Alsacian cuisine is a major tourist attraction in itself. Bernard's restaurant in Hotel Le Rapp is my dress-up, high-cuisine splurge of the tour ($10). I comb my hair, change my socks and savor a slow, elegant meal served with grace and fine wine. Why not? Don't miss the "Salad Rapp." For crepes with atmosphere— **Creperie Tom Pouce**, 10 Rue des Tanneurs, tel. 232700. For cheap. low-risk, low-stress meals eat at the **Flunch** self-service on Place Rapp or in the fine cafeteria at Monoprix near the Unterlinden Museum

Itinerary Options

If the weather is bad, or you happen to hate mountains, try this: The Lauterbrunnen-Interlaken train ($3, 30 minutes, goes frequently) will zip you into the big town resort of the region. Interlaken has lots of resorty activities and shopping. At the other end of Lake Brienz is Switzerland's best open-air folk museum, Ballenberg (open 9 am-5:30 pm daily). It's the best possible look at Swiss folk life, with old traditional buildings from all over the country gathered together displaying the old culture.

From the Cinqueterre you could trade Switzerland for France and spend a day in Nice, Cannes and Monte Carlo. Take the night train to Chamonix for the best of the French Alps (Mont Blanc) and take the night-train (12 am-8 pm) directly into Paris from there. This plan is much better by train than by car.

From Interlaken you can also do minor surgery on your itinerary, skip Alsace entirely, and go directly to Paris (excellent overnight train or all-day drive).

If you're not really interested in France it would be interesting to mosey back to Amsterdam via more of Switzerland, the Bodensee, the Black Forest, Trier, Mosel Valley, Luxembourg, Brussels and Bruges. This is mostly small-town and countryside travel so it's best for car travelers.

Or, you may decide to sell your plane ticket and permanently join Heidi and the cows waiting for eternity in Europe's greatest cathedral—the Swiss Alps.

France

■ 210,000 square miles (Europe's largest country, Texas-sized).
■ 55 million people (248 per square mile, 78 percent urban).
■ You may have heard that the French are mean and cold. Don't believe it. If anything, they're pouting because they're no longer the world's premier culture. It's tough to be crushed by a Big Mac and keep on smiling. Be sensitive and understanding. The French are cold only if you choose to perceive them that way. Look for friendliness, give people the benefit of the doubt,

respect all that's French and you'll remember France with a smile.
■ Formerly the world's most powerful country, France has
much to offer in so many ways. Paris will overwhelm you if you
don't do a little studying. And Paris is just the beginning of
Europe's largest and most diverse country.
■ Learn some French—at least the polite words—and try to
sound like Maurice Chevalier. The French don't speak much
English—but they speak much more English than we speak
French. Unless you speak French, you'll have to be patient
about any communications problems.
■ The French are experts in the art of fine living. Their cuisine,
their customs, even their vacationing habits, are highly devel-
oped. Since the vacation is such a big part of the French life-
style (nearly every worker takes either July or August off), you'll
find no shortage of tourist information centers, hotels, transportation facilities and fun ways to pass free days.
■ The French eat lunch from 12 pm to 2 pm, dinner from 7 pm
to 10 pm—and eat well. Each region has its high cuisine specialties and even the "low cuisine" of a picnic can be elegant, with
fresh bread and an endless variety of tasty French cheeses,
meats, rich pastries and, of course, wine. The best approach to
French food is to eat where locals eat and be adventurous. Eat
ugly things with relish!
■ The French government takes pride in its independence
from the USA, USSR, Britain, Germany, and the Church. While
the French per capita income is respectable, and while the nation leads Europe in farm production, France's economy under
its socialist government has gone very flat. France has a large
poor class (the poorest 20 percent of the people have only 2
percent of the wealth) and the French franc has sunk to record
lows. A few years ago there were four francs to a dollar. At the
time of this writing there are over seven.
■ France is a reasonably-priced place to travel (plenty of $18
double rooms) and a shopper's delight. Visitors are consistently
lured away from important sights by important savings on luxury items, high fashions, perfume, antiques and tourist trinkets
ranging from glow-in-the-dark necklaces to fake gargoyles.

DAY 20

COLMAR, ALSACIAN VILLAGES, WINE TASTING

After a Bernard breakfast, spend the morning exploring Colmar. After a late lunch at Flunch (a great French self-serve cafeteria chain) go into the countryside to wander the Route du Vin (wine road) and visit the villages of Eguisheim and Kaysersberg. Drop by a winery in either town for a tour and tasting (but the nearby Bennwihr Cooperative has the best tour) before returning to Hotel Le Rapp for dinner. Try to sample Cremant, the Alsace's version of champagne—it's very good and much cheaper.

Suggested Schedule	
8:00 am	Breakfast.
8:30 am	Orientation walk, ending at tourist office.
9:00 am	Unterlinden Museum.
10:30 am	Free time to shop, sightsee, wash or mail.
1:00 pm	Lunch at Flunch or picnic in a village.
2:00 pm	Exploration of wine road and villages.
7:30 pm	Dinner, Hotel Le Rapp.

Sightseeing Highlights
▲▲▲**Unterlinden Museum**—Colmar's touristic claim to fame, this is one of my favorite museums in Europe. While its collection ranges from Roman Colmar to medieval wine-making exhibits to traditional wedding dresses to babies' cribs to Picasso, Grunewald's gripping Isenheim Altarpiece deserves top billing. Pick up the English guidebook at the desk, study the polyptych model of the multi-paneled painting on the wall next to the original, and get acquainted with this greatest of late-medieval German masterpieces. Open 9-6 daily.
▲▲**Dominican Church**—This is another medieval mind-blower that awaits your attention. In the Dominican church you'll find Martin Schongauer's angelically beautiful Madonna of the Roses, looking like it was painted yesterday, holding court on center stage (open 10-6 daily). On many evenings you can enjoy its 13th century stained glass lit from inside.
Tanner's Quarters—This refurbished chunk of the old town is a delight, day or night. Don't miss the creperie at 10 Rue des Tanneurs.
Bartholdi Museum—An interesting little museum about the life and work of the local boy who gained fame by sculpting

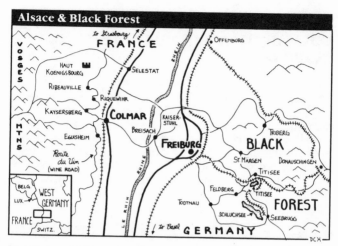

our Statue of Liberty. You'll notice several of his statues, usually
with one arm raised high, gracing Colmar's squares.

Route du Vin Sidetrip

Alsace has so much to offer. If you have only one afternoon,
limit yourself to these two towns:

Eguisheim—Just a few miles from Colmar, this scenic little
town is best explored by walking around its circular road, then
cutting through the middle. Visit the Eguisheim Wine Cooperative. You may have to wait for a group to enjoy their free tour.

Kaysersberg—Albert Schweitzer's hometown is larger but just
as cute as Eguisheim. Climb the castle, browse through the art
galleries, taste some wine (*degustation* means "come on in and
taste," *gratuit* means "free," otherwise there is a very small
charge.) and wander along nearby vineyards.

By car this is easy. Otherwise buses are possible, but I'd
recommend renting a bike at the Colmar station for your wine
road excursion (go easy on the tasting).

Helpful Hints

Old Colmar is easily covered on foot. Worthwhile guidebooks
are in most gift shops and the tourist office can provide maps,
hours, a private guide ($25), and general information and ideas
for your trip into the wine road region.

Colmar is a good place for mailing things if your parcel is
under 10 pounds. (Paris is a headache.) The post office near
Place Rapp sells boxes, is open 8 am-7 pm, and is a good place
to lighten your load. Colmar is also a good place to do laundry
and to shop (laundromat in Petite Venise, daily 8 am-9 pm,
stores close Monday mornings).

DAY 21
THE LONG DRIVE TO PARIS, STOPPING AT REIMS

Today's journey will take you halfway across France to Paris, with a stop for lunch, a champagne tour and visit to the great Gothic cathedral in Reims. You'll be in Paris in time for dinner, a subway lesson and a city orientation tour.

Suggested Schedule	
7:00	Leave Colmar. Breakfast at rest stop.
12:00	Reims—picnic, tour cathedral and Champagne cave.
2:00	Drive to Paris.
5:00	Set up in Paris.

Transportation
Drivers should leave Colmar by 7:30 am, head north past Strasbourg and take the autobahn straight to Reims (5 hours). You'll pass Verdun (an interesting stop for history and WWI buffs) and lots of strange (and silly) modern Franco-freeway art.

Take the Reims exit marked "Cathedral" and you'll see your destination. Park near the church. Picnic in the park near its front (public w.c., dangerous grass, glorious setting).

Back on the freeway, it's a straight shot (excepting toll booth stops) into Paris. By this schedule, you should hit it just about rush hour (No tour is perfect).

If you're renting a car it would be handy, if possible, to turn it in at the Charles de Gaulle airport and take the bus or subway into town. Or call your hotel from Reims and ask if you can arrive late. Or just damn the torpedoes, think of it as San Francisco or Boston, fasten your seatbelt, check your insurance, and drive. If you're in danger of going "in-Seine," hire a cab and follow him to your hotel. If you think you're good behind the wheel, drive this introductory tour as the sun sets: go over the Austerlitz Bridge, to the Luxembourg Gardens, down Boulevard St. Michel, past Notre Dame on the island, up Rue Champs-Elysees, around the Arc de Triomphe (6 or 8 giggly times) and to your hotel. (Confirm your hotel reservation upon arrival or earlier in the day by telephone.)

By train you can connect from Colmar to Reims to Paris easily, but I'd probably skip Reims, save a day, and take the train overnight direct to Paris. Chartres Cathedral, an hour's side trip from Paris is as good as Reims.

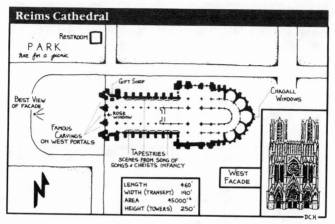

Reims Cathedral

PARK
nice for a picnic

RESTROOM

GIFT SHOP

ROSE WINDOW

BEST VIEW OF FACADE

FAMOUS CARVINGS ON WEST PORTALS

TAPESTRIES
SCENES FROM SONG OF SONGS & CHRISTS INFANCY

CHAGALL WINDOWS

WEST FACADE

LENGTH	460'
WIDTH (TRANSEPT)	190'
AREA	45000'²
HEIGHT (TOWERS)	250'

—DCH

Reims

The cathedral of Reims is one of the best examples of Gothic architecture you'll see. Its front end is considered the best west portal anywhere, and for 800 years it was the coronation place of French kings and queens. It houses many old treasures, not to mention a lovely set of Marc Chagall stained glass windows. Take this opportunity to fall in love with Gothic. (Open 8 am to 9 pm daily.)

Reims is the capital of the Champagne region and, while the bubbly stuff's birthplace was Epernay, it's best to save nearly two hours of road time by touring a Champagne cave right in Reims. Walk 10 minutes up Rue de Barbatre from the Cathedral to #9 Place St. Nicaise (tel. 85-4535) where the Taittinger Company will do a great job trying to convince you they're the best. After seeing their movie (the comfy theater seats alone make this a worthwhile visit), follow your guide down into some of the three miles of chilly chalk caves, many dug by ancient Romans. Popping corks signal when the tour's done and the tasting's begun.

One block beyond Taittinger, on Place des Droits de l'Homme, you'll find several other Champagne firms. Most give free tours from 9-11 am and 2-5 pm. I'd recommend Piper Heidsieck with a tacky train ride tour (51 Blvd. Henry-Vasnier, tel. 85-0194) and Veuve Clicquot-Pousardin (#1 Place des Droits de l'Homme, tel. 85-2568). If you want to drive to Epernay (nice town, plenty of cheap hotels) the best Champagne firm with the best tours is right downtown—Moet Chandon.

DAY 22

PARIS

Take a day to cover the core sights of Paris and get comfortable with the city in general.

Start by subwaying to the St. Michel stop where you'll emerge in the heart of an uncharacteristically sleepy Latin Quarter. This is a street-hoppin' place at night; it uses mornings to recover. Walk down rue de la Huchette (past my favorite jazz cellar at #5—check the schedule) and over the bridge to Notre Dame cathedral. It took 200 years to build this church. Tour it accordingly. Walking through the center of the island, Ile de la Cite, you'll come to the Sainte-Chapelle church, newly restored, a Gothic gem. Walk to the tip of the island (lovely park) and cross the oldest bridge in town, the Pont Neuf. In Paris, like Rome, be on guard for gypsy kids who tug on your heart strings and your purse strings simultaneously. On your left, across the Pont Neuf, is to Samaritaine department store. Have lunch on its 5th floor (cafeteria opens at 11:35). Then your time has come to tackle the Louvre, at one time Europe's grandest palace and biggest building and still its greatest—and most overwhelming—museum. Walk down the riverside wall past a door which is often open and strangely unused. If you see an open door on the riverside wall enter there, otherwise go around the corner and join the mob. The line moves quickly and it's well worth the wait. Buy a combination guided tour-admission ticket. A tour is the best way to enjoy this huge museum. If you have to wait for an English tour, get the square little Louvre book and study it, or browse through the books and cards.

If you are unable to get a guide, a good do-it-yourself tour of the museum's highlights would include: ancient Greek, Parthenon frieze, Venus de Milo, Nike of Samothrace, Apollo Gallery (jewels, opens at 2:00), French paintings found between the Nike of Samothrace and the Grande Galerie, the Grande Galerie (a quarter of a mile long and worth the hike), the Mona Lisa and the rest of the works in that room, the nearby Neo-classical collection (Coronation of Napoleon, David) and the Romantic collection (Delacroix and Gericault) in that order.

For the rest of the afternoon, I'd recommend a walk up the Champs-Elysees to the Arc de Triomphe.

Suggested Schedule

8:00 am	Breakfast.
8:30 am	Subway to St. Michel in Latin Quarter.
9:00 am	Walk through Latin Quarter to Notre Dame.
9:30 am	Tour Notre Dame.
10:00 am	Deportation Memorial
10:30 am	Tour Ste. Chapelle.
11:30 am	Lunch at 5th floor Samaritaine dept. store, self-service, panorama from rooftop.
1:00 pm	Tour the Louvre, hopefully with a guide.
3:00 pm	Options: Orsay Museum, Rodin Museum; Hike up Champs-Elysees; Napoleon's Tomb, Les Halles.
7:30 pm	Dinner.
9:00 pm	Evening on Montmartre.

Sightseeing Highlights

▲▲**Latin Quarter**—This area lies between the Luxembourg Gardens and the island centering around the Sorbonne university and Boulevards St. Germain and St. Michel. This is the core of the Left Bank—the artsy, liberal, hippie, Bohemian, poet and philosopher district full of international eateries, far-out book shops, street singers and jazz clubs. For colorful wandering and cafe-sitting, afternoons and evenings are best.

▲▲ **Notre Dame Cathedral**—700 years old, packed with history and tourists. Climb to the top (entrance on outside left) for a great view.   Get close to a gargoyle. Study its sculpture (the Notre Dame's forte) and windows, take in a musical service (much more beautiful than the touristic organ recitals), eavesdrop on guides, walk all around the outside. Open 8-7. Free tours are normally at 10:45, 11:45, 2:30, 3:30, 4:30 and 5:30 pm. Treasury open 10-6. Take stairs to top, open 10-5:30. Don't miss the powerful memorial to the French victims of the holocaust (on the tip of the island near Ille St. Louis, behind the Notre Dame—opens at 10:00, free).

▲▲▲**Sainte-Chapelle**—The triumph of Gothic church architecture, a cathedral of glass, like none other. It was built in just 33 months to house the crown of thorns—which cost the king more than the church. Newly restored. Good little black book in English available. Open 10-6. Concerts almost every evening. Even a beginning violin class would sound lovely in that atmospheric room.

▲▲▲**The Louvre**—Europe's oldest, biggest, greatest, and maybe most crowded museum. Take a tour. Buy the square little guidebook. Don't try to cover it thoroughly. Open 9:45-6:30 (some sections close 11:30-2:00). Closed Tuesday. Free (and more crowded) on Sunday. Tel. info 42603926. English tours normally leave at 10:15, 11:30 and 3:30.

▲▲ **Orsay Museum**—The impressionist art of the now-closed Jeu de Paume is combined with several other art collections in Paris' long-awaited 19th century art museum. Located just across the river from the old Jeu de Paume in a former train station.

▲**Napoleon's Tomb** and **Les Invalides**—The Emperor lies majestically dead under a grand dome—a goose-bumping pilgrimage for historians—surrounded by Europe's greatest military museum. Open daily 10-6.

▲**Rodin Museum**—Work of the greatest sculptor since Michelangelo.   This museum is filled with surprisingly entertaining sculpture: The Kiss, The Thinker, and many more. Just across the street from Napoleon's Tomb. (Open 10-6, closed Tuesdays.)

▲**Pompidou Center**—This controversial, colorfully exoskeletal building houses Europe's greatest collection of far-out modern art, the Musee National d'Art Moderne. You'll find fun art such as a piano smashed to bits and glued to the wall, and much more. It is a social center with lots of people. There's activity inside and out, swamped by a perpetual street fair. (Open Noon-10 pm, Sat. and Sun. 10-10, closed Tuesdays, free on Sunday.)

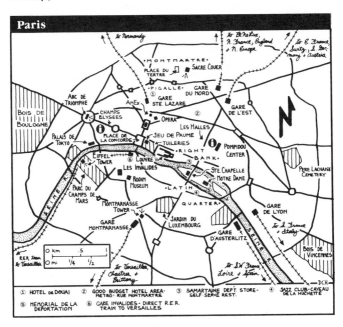

Paris

① HOTEL de DOUAI   ② GOOD BUDGET HOTEL AREA·
                         METRO· RUE MONTMARTRE
③ SAMARITAINE DEPT. STORE·
   SELF-SERVE REST.
④ JAZZ CLUB· CAVEAU
   DE LA HUCHETTE
⑤ MEMORIAL DE LA
   DEPORTATION
⑥ GARE INVALIDES· DIRECT R.E.R.
   TRAIN TO VERSAILLES

▲▲**Eiffel Tower**—Crowded and expensive, but worth the trouble. Open daily 9:30 am-midnight. Heck of a view.

▲▲**Montparnasse Tower**—59-floor superscraper, cheaper and easier to get to the top than the Eiffel Tower. Paris' best view. Buy the photo-guide to the city, go to the rooftop and orient yourself. This is the best way to understand the lay of this magnificent land. It's a good place to be as the sun goes down on your first day in Paris. Find your hotel, retrace your day's steps, locate the famous buildings. Open 9:30 am-11:30 pm.

▲**Samaritaine Department Store Viewpoint**—Go to the rooftop. Quiz yourself. Turn counter-clockwise, identifying the Eiffel Tower, Invalides, Napoleon's Tomb, Montparnasse, Henry IV on the island, Sorbonne, Pantheon, Ste. Chapelle, Hotel de Ville, Pompidou Centre, Sacre Couer, Opera and Louvre.

▲▲**Sacre Coeur and Montmartre**—The Byzantine-looking church is only 100 years old (built as a praise-the-Lord-anyway gesture after the French were humiliated by the Germans in a brief war) but it's very impressive. Nearby is the Place du Tertre, the haunt of Toulouse-Lautrec and home of the original "Bohemians." Today it's mobbed by tourists, but still fun. Watch the artists, tip the street singers, have a dessert crepe. Church is open daily and evenings.

Seine River Tour—A relaxing, if uninspiring, trip up and down the river past all the famous buildings, costs $3, leaves from the Pont Neuf or near the Eiffel Tower.

Best Shopping—Forum Halles is a grand new subterranean center. A sight in itself. Fun, mod, colorful, very Parisian. The Lafayette Galleries behind the Opera House is your best elegant, old-world one-stop Parisian department-store shopping center. Samaritaine department store near Pont Neuf.

Pigalle—Paris' red light district. More shocking than dangerous if you stick to the bigger streets, hang onto your wallet and exercise good judgment.

Sidetrips

▲▲▲**Versailles**—Europe's palace of palaces, Versailles is 12 miles from downtown Paris. To get there take the subway to "Invalides" and follow signs to "Versailles R.G." Ride that train ($1, free with Eurail, 45 minutes; runs every ten minutes) to the end of the line (Versailles R.G.) and walk ten minutes to the palace. Arrive before 9:45 am to avoid the mob scene. Tour groups arrive after 11 am. Tuesdays are the most crowded. Take the private "king's apartments" tour immediately to avoid more crowds (use Guided Tour entrance—see map). Buy the middle-priced guide book for a room-by-room rundown. Walk 45

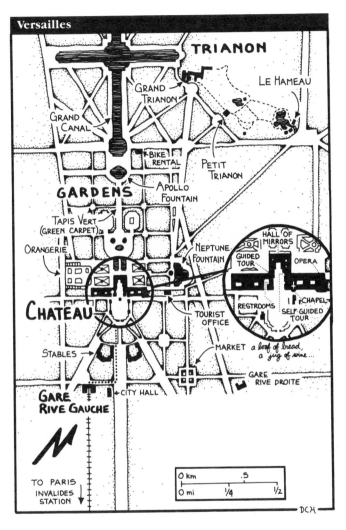

minutes (or rent a bike) to the Little Hamlet if possible; it's a
great picnic spot. Open Tues.-Sun. 9:45-5:30, closed Monday.
   ▲**Chartres**—One of Europe's most important Gothic cathedrals,
one hour by train from Paris. Open 7 am-7 pm. Malcolm Miller
gives great "Appreciation of Gothic" tours every day (except
Sunday) at noon and 2:45 pm. Each tour is different. Just show
up at the church. This church is great, but for most people
Notre Dame in Downtown Paris is easier and good enough.

Chartres has a good youth hostel with a fabulous cathedral view.
Giverny—Monet's garden is very popular with his fans. Open 10-12, 2-6, April 1-Oct. 31, closed Monday. Take Rouen train from St. Lazare Station to Vernon, then walk, hitch or taxi to Giverny.

Helpful Hints
Remember, nearly all Paris museums are closed on Tuesdays. Pick up a copy of the weekly entertainment guide, "Pariscope," at a newsstand to check the local museum hours and know what's going on at night. There's a great jazz club scene and dancing at the **Caveau de la Huchette** (5 Rue de la Huchette) in the Latin Quarter. Note that Paris expanded its overworked phone system, adding a 4 to the beginning of all old numbers. Pick up the handy free city and subway map of Paris at any hotel.

The Paris Metro is Europe's best subway system. One ticket takes you anywhere much faster than a car or cab for 50 cents. Buy tickets in books of ten (*carnet*) for big savings. Most addresses include the *arrondisement* (district) number as well as the nearest subway stop. (i.e. "Mo: Montmartre" means near the Montmartre subway stop.) It's easy if you have a map and know that *sortie* means exit and *correspondence* means "go this way to make a connection." Directions are indicated by the last stop on that line.

If possible, use the RER system. It's much, much faster, subway tickets are accepted ideal for connecting Paris' train stations and getting out to Versailles. While subways are faster, Parisian buses are great for joy riding. Buses 21, 69, 95, and 96 are each very scenic.

Food and Lodging
Finding rooms in Paris is most difficult in September, which is convention month. July and August are fairly easy—just don't look for hotels in the shadows of famous buildings. Take the subway to any neighborhood that you've never heard of, walk down the street, and find your own special one- or two-star (blue-and-white plaque) hotel offering doubles with breakfast and a smile for $20. Note: a shower in your room will generally add $15 to the price. Arrive early or use one of the tourist office room-finding services (tel. 43-591212).

A handy, quiet, central and safe neighborhood with a cluster of fine budget hotels is at the Metro (subway) stop, Montmartre (in the ninth district, halfway between the Opera and the Pompidou Center). Find the quiet alley running between Rue

Bergere and Boulevard Poissonniere (30 yards in front of the Flunch and through a corridor on the left).

My Montmartre recommendations:

1. **Hotel des Arts** (7 Cite Bergere, 75009 Paris. tel. 4246-7330, $40 doubles with showers, classy, some English spoken, friendly.)

2. **Hotel Cite Rougemont** (4 Cite Rougemont, 75009 Paris. tel. 4770-2595 $20 doubles w/o shower, some English, friendly, fun.)

3. Several cheaper ($20 doubles, not so clean, but acceptable—cleanliness and character often ride the same teeter-totter): **Hotel Comprador** (2 Cite Rougemont, tel. 4770-4442); **Hotel Rex** (4 Cite Rougemont, tel. 4824-6071, English spoken, the manager has ties with several hotels and can normally get you a bed.); **Hotel d'Espagne** (9 Cite Bergere, tel. 4770-1394).

Other areas:

Hotel de Douai (32 Rue de Douai, 75009 Paris, tel. 4874-4867). People love it or hate it. Bubbles with character on edge of red light district and seedy side roads. One block from Moulin Rouge (Metro stop: Blanche). $20 doubles. Jane, the night-watch lady, writes upside down and will happily talk your ears off, especially if you are interested in the Celtic struggles of Brittany. **Hotel Daguerre** (94 Rue Daguerre, 75014 Paris, tel. 4322-4354, near Metro stop: Guite, off Ave du Marne) is reasonable, comfy, English-speaking, and in a great locale near Montparnasse Tower. **Hotel International** (6 Rue Auguste-Barbier, Metro: Goncourt, 75011 Paris, tel. 14-357-3807) is also very good but a bit more expensive, $35 doubles.

There are plenty of reasonable hotels near the Arc-de-Triomphe, another great locale. Try the **Star Hotel** (18 Rue de L'Arc de Triomphe,75017 Paris, tel. 4380-2769, between Ave Carnot and Ave MacMahon, $30 doubles) or **Hotel Elysee** (5 Rue de L'Etoile, 75017 Paris, tel. 4380-2219, classy, $40 doubles). In the Latin Quarter look for cheap decent rooms along Rue des Ecoles. Student travelers should take advantage of the room-finding service at 119 Rue St. Martin near the Pompidou Center, tel. 42778780, at the Gare du Nord, at 16 Rue du Pont Louis Philippe near the Hotel du Ville, or at 139 Blvd. St. Michel in the Latin Quarter.

You could eat yourself silly in Paris. The city could hold a gourmet's Olympics—and import nothing. I picnic or self-serve it for quick lunches and linger longer over delicious dinners. You can eat very well, restaurant style, for $8. Ask your hotel to recommend a small, French restaurant nearby in the 50 to 80-franc range. Famous places are overpriced, overcrowded and usually overrated. Find a quiet neighborhood and wander or follow a local recommendation. You'll dine fine.

Self-serve recommendations: There are plenty. Check department store top floors (Samaritaine at Pont Neuf near Louvre). **Flunch** has branches near most of the hotels I recommended (just coincidence), and on Champs-Elysees.

Small, family-style Parisian restaurant favorites: **La Petite Bouclerie** (33 Rue de la Harpe, in Latin Quarter). This has family cooking with class on busy, fun, if over-touristed street $10. **Au Fleuri** (51 Rue Blanche, down the street from recommended Hotel de Douai) is very local-style with self-service prices. **Restaurant Polidar** (41 Rue Monsieur le Prince, Metro: Odeon) is popular, crowded, cheap and worth the wait. **Restaurant Chez Fernandez** (17 Rue de la Fontaine au Roi, Metro: Goncourt) is local and homey as they come—with great Beaujolais. And all along Rue Mouffetard you'll find good intimate, reasonable dining with after-dinner music. **Le Clas Descarts** at 8 Rue Descarts (tel. 432-54494) just off Rou Mouffetard (Metro: Monge) serves wonderful $7 meals.

For good Vietnamese food try **Restaurant Hawai** (daily 10 to 3, 6 to 10, tel. 4586-9190, 87 Ave d'Ivry, metro: d'Ivry, several others nearby). **Restaurant le Drouet** (51 Rue du Commerce) and the **Butte en Vigne** (Vamp atmosphere, 5 Rue Poulbot, 75018 Paris, tel 4606-9196, in Montmartre district) are also good. A great working class favorite near the Arc de Triomphe is **L'Etoile Verte** (the Green Star), 13 Rue Brey, metro: Etoile, tel. 4380-6934.

For a classy picnic, shop at Paris' famous Fauchon. This food store elevates window displays to a fine art (looking is free, located just behind the Madeleine).

And for crazy (but quite touristy) cellar atmosphere and hearty fun food, don't miss a feast at **La Taverne du Sergent Recruiter** (the "Sergeant Recruiter" used to get young Parisians drunk and stuffed here and then signed them into the army), center of Ille St. Louis, 3 minutes from Notre Dame, 41 Rue St. Louis, open Mon.-Sat. 7:00 to 2:00, tel. 4354-7542, all you can eat for 120 francs including wine and service.

* * *

That's my idea of the best 22 days Europe has to offer. Bon voyage et bonne chance!

POST-TOUR OPTIONS

Okay, depending on how much time and money you've got,
now you can choose from these options:

1. Return home from Amsterdam where you landed ($40 train
ride, five hours from Paris). Hopefully, you thought ahead on
the first day and booked a room for your last night in Holland.
Remember to confirm your flight by phone three days before
you leave.

2. Mosey back to Amsterdam, stopping at Brussels and
wonderful Brugge on the way and maybe rent a bike to explore
a bit of Holland or Belgium before D-Day (departure).

3. Return to Amsterdam via London. Overnight train from Paris
to London and then London to Amsterdam. The boat is figured
into the train ride, so don't worry about it. It's $40 each way
($30 overnight).

4. More time in England? Rent a car ($100/week including
mileage) at the airport to avoid London traffic nightmares.

5. More side trips from Paris before returning to Amsterdam.
Consider the Loire Valley (near Tours), two hours south of Paris.
Great towns and castles. Or, Normandy and Brittany with
Rouen, Mont St.-Michel, Bayeux and lots more.

6. Before your trip ask your agent about "open-jaws" return
flights. You could fly home from Paris, London, Ireland, Lisbon,
Athens or even Bombay!

7. For a larger extension of your tour consider a Eurail adventure in Scandanavia, Iberia, or a trip down to the Greek Isles.

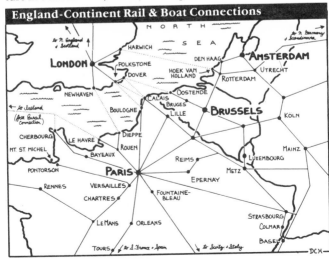

LONDON

London is this itinerary's greatest omission. You could easily start and end your tour here with a few extra days. From Paris you can take the train/boat trip. Overnight is cheaper and will save you a day. The trip takes about eight hours. If you have a Sea-Link Britrail coupon, buy only the train ticket to the coast, as the boat is covered. The Hovercraft is faster but costs more and you lose the cruise flavor. The normal boat ride is more relaxing and scenic. The train meets the boat, and two hours later you're in Victoria Station, London. You should have reserved your bed from Paris or earlier by phone.

Upon arrival, buy your ticket to Amsterdam (in train station), stop by the station's tourist info office, then take the subway to your accommodations.

Orientation

London, over 600 square miles of urban jungle with seven million struggling people, is a world in itself, a barrage on all the senses, and a place that can make you feel very small. It's much more than museums and famous landmarks. It's a living, breathing organism that somehow manages to thrive.

London Town has changed dramatically in recent years and many visitors are surprised to find how "un-English" it is. Whites are actually a minority now in a city that once symbolized white imperialism. Arabs have pretty much bought out the area north of Hyde Park. Fish and chips shops are now outnumbered by Chinese take-outs. Most hotels are run or at least staffed by people with foreign accents, while outlying suburbs are huge communities of Jamaicans, Pakistanis, Indians and Orientals. London is learning—sometimes fitfully—to live as a microcosm of its formerly vast empire.

With just three nights and two days here you'll get no more than a quick splash in this teeming human tidepool. But hopefully, with some quick orientation, you'll get a good sampling of its top sights, history, cultural entertainment and ever-changing human face.

London has all the pitfalls of any big city, but if you're on the ball, informed and well-organized it won't cost a fortune, you won't get ripped-off, and you'll leave ready for the more peaceful countryside but looking forward to your return.

Transportation in London

London's taxis, buses and subway system make a private car unnecessary. In a city this size, you must get comfortable with its public transportation. Don't be timid; dive in, figure it out, and in no time you'll have London by the tail.

Taxis—Big, black, carefully regulated cabs are everywhere. I've never met a crabby cabbie in London. They love to talk and know every nook and cranny in town. Rides start at 70p and stay surprisingly reasonable. There are often extra charges (legitimate ones) added on, but usually two or three people in a cab travel at subway prices. If the top light is on just wave one down. Telephoning is unnecessary—taxis are everywhere.

Buses—London's extensive bus system is easy to follow if you have a map listing the routes (as on most tourist maps). Signs at the stops list exactly where the buses go, and conductors are terse but helpful. Ask to be reminded when it's your stop. Just hop on and take a seat (I always go upstairs). You'll be ticketed whenever the conductor gets around to it. Buses and taxis are miserable during rush hours—8-10 am and 4-7 pm. Rides vary from 30p to over a pound.

Subway—The London "tube" is one of this planet's great people movers. Every city map includes a tube map. You'll need it. Navigate by color-coded lines and north (always up on the map) south, east or west. You buy your ticket before descending—at the window or from coin-op machines to avoid the line—then hang onto it, giving it to a checker as you leave the system. Read system notices and signs carefully, ask questions of locals, and watch your wallet. You'll find that "tubing" is by far the fastest long-distance transport in town. It used to be fiercely expensive but now is a reasonable 30 pence to 1.50 pounds per ride.

Special Money-Saving Transit Tickets

Nearly every tourist should take advantage of one of these subway/bus "go as you please" specials. Available on the spot in subway stations, they give you unlimited transportation on all buses and subways.

Explorer Pass—1 day-3 pounds, 3 days 8.50 pounds, 4 days-11 pounds, and 7 days-14 pounds, covering the entire system including subway and Airbus to and from Heathrow airport.

Travelcard—7 days unlimited coverage within the subway "circle" line for 4 pounds. Few tourists take advantage of this, though nearly every major tourist sight is covered in this central circle. The airport trip, unfortunately, isn't covered. Pick this card up in any subway station (photo required). Travelcards are available covering bigger areas and longer durations.

Cheap day returns—The English love to encourage round trips on train, subway or bus with R/T fares often just barely more than one-way.

Ask at any tube station for a brochure about special passes.

It makes negative sense to prepurchase any of these in the USA. But wise travelers pick them up upon arrival to cover the ride in from Heathrow.

London Information

You can't do London without information. Good guidebooks abound. (I like *Let's Go Britain* and London guides by Michelin, Beazley, and Frommer.) The free London transport and tourist map (available at the Tourist Information office, some subway stations and hotels) is good enough, but the first class map (50p) is ideal.

Tourist offices are located at Heathrow airport, in Victoria Station (tel. 730-3488, open daily 9:00-8:30, 8:00-10:00 in July and August), at Selfridges on Oxford Street and at Harrods (regular store hours). The Victoria Station office has a great selection of books covering all of Britain, a room-finding service (not cheap), and a helpful staff with a huge arsenal of fliers, lists, maps and printed advice. They can also sell you theater tickets.

For the best listing of what's going on this week (plays, movies, exhibitions, concerts, walking tours, protests, what to do with children, restaurants, etc.) pick up a current copy of "What's On"-80p at any newsstand. ("Time Out" and "City Limits" are hip and more opinionated versions of "What's On".) You can also telephone 246-8041 for a taped listing of today's happenings.

At the tourist info desk, have a check list. Go over your London plans, buy a ticket to a play, and pick up these publications:

Events and Entertainment, theater guide
"What's On" (or "Time Out" or "City Limits")
Quick Guide to London-50p.

Two Days In London

The sights of London alone could easily fill a book like this. Let's spend two days enjoying as many of these sights as time and energy will allow.

Suggested Schedule

Day 1

8:00 am	Breakfast, subway or bus to Marble Arch.
9:00 am	Catch Round London Tour.
11:00 am	Taxi to Buckingham Palace for 11:00 Changing of the Guard. Or practice a little urban immersion—strolling, window-shopping and people watching your way from Marble Arch along Oxford Street, Regent Street, Soho, Piccadilly and Leicester Square to Covent Gardens.
1:00 pm	Lunch in Covent Gardens—no shortage of intriguing food and colorful surroundings.
2:00 pm	Walk the Strand to the Temple Tube station and subway to Tower Hill. Tour the Tower of London starting with the Beefeater Tour. Don't miss the crown jewels.
5:00 pm	Sail from the Tower to Westminster Bridge enjoying a thirty-minute commentary on the Thames. Westminster Abbey is open until 6:00 and the Visitors Gallery in the Halls of Parliament is open, when in session, from 6:00 pm. (If you have a play to see or are traveling in summer, this schedule is probably too much unless you're real speedy.)
7:00 pm	Pub dinner near your theater.
8:00 pm	Most plays start at 8:00 pm, enjoy the one of your choice.

Day 2

8:00 am	Breakfast, easy morning. Subway to Tottenham Court Rd.
10:00 am	British Museum.
1:30 pm	Pub lunch on Fleet Street, London's frantic but dignified newspaper and print center. Or for a light healthier meal, try "Slender's Wholefood Restaurant" at 41 Cathedral Place, near St. Paul's.
2:00 pm	Walk to St. Paul's, climb to top for view. Many other Wren churches nearby, as well as Old Bailey and the Stock Exchange.
4:00 pm	Walk to The Museum of London (open till 6:00 pm) for the best possible London history lesson.
Evening	Hopefully a performance (music or Royal Shakespeare Co.) in the new and impressive Barbican Center a block from the London Museum. (Open until 11:00 pm daily, tel. info 638-4141 ext. 218, recorded info 628-2295).

Accommodations

Cheap, central and comfortable—pick two. With London's great subways, I'll sacrifice centrality for a cheery place that won't ruin my budget. London has hundreds of hotels but few great deals. There's no need, however, to spend a fortune or stay in a dangerous, depressing dump.

Reserve your London room in advance with a phone call direct from the states. Assure them that you'll arrive before 4:00 pm, or send a signed travelers check covering at least the first night. (Include a note explaining that you'll be happy to pay cash upon arrival so they can avoid bank charges if they'll just hold your check until you get there.)

Here are a few of my favorites:

Hotel Ravna Gora—Located just across from the Holland Park tube station. Formerly Mr. Holland's mansion, now it's a large B&B run by supporters of the long-exiled King of Yugoslavia. Eccentric and well worn—still, you won't find a more comfortable or handy place for the price. Manda and Rijko take care of their guests while downstairs the Serbian royalists quaff beer and dream of a glorious restoration some day. Royal TV room, good English breakfast, on the Central tube line, Airbus A2 uphill from Kensington Hilton. Single-15 pounds, Double-22 pounds, Triple-30 pounds, Quads-40 pounds. At 29 Holland Park Avenue, London WII, tel. 727-7725.

Vicarage Private Hotel, 10 Vicarage Gate, Kensington, London W8, tel. 229-4030, is very popular, family-run in a quiet, classy neighborhood midway between Notting Hill Gate and High Street Kensington tube stations near Kensington Palace. Smaller, cozier and more expensive than Ravna Gora. Prices with English breakfast and shower down the hall are: Single-15 pounds, Double-26 pounds, Triple-33 pounds, Quad-37 pounds. Make reservations long in advance with phone call followed by one night's deposit (travelers checks in pounds).

Abbey House Hotel, 11 Vicarage Gate, Kensington, London, W8, tel. 727-2594 is similar in almost every way to its neighbor the Vicarage Private Hotel. A few pounds more expensive. Friendly management. One night deposit required ($50 signed travelers check is fine).

Alba Guest House, 53 Pembridge Villas, London, W11, tel. 727-8910 is very small, friendly and family run in a funky but pleasant locale at the foot of colorful Portobello Road, a block from the Nottinghill subway stop. Run by Raymond Khoo, 26 pound doubles.

Methodist International House—at 4 Inverness Terrace near Bayswater tube, tel. 229-5101. This Christian residence filled

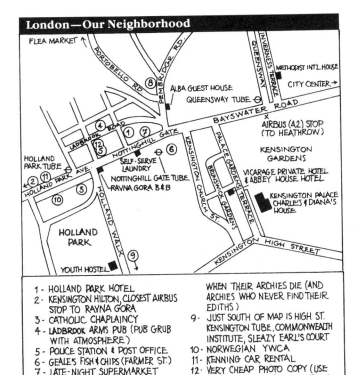

London—Our Neighborhood

1 - HOLLAND PARK HOTEL
2 - KENSINGTON HILTON, CLOSEST AIRBUS STOP TO RAYNA GORA
3 - CATHOLIC CHAPLAINCY
4 - LADBROOK ARMS PUB (PUB GRUB WITH ATMOSPHERE)
5 - POLICE STATION & POST OFFICE
6 - GEALE'S FISH & CHIPS (FARMER ST.)
7 - LATE-NIGHT SUPERMARKET
8 - GALLEON RESTAURANT - VERY CHEAP. WHERE EDITH BUNKERS GO

WHEN THEIR ARCHIES DIE (AND ARCHIES WHO NEVER FIND THEIR EDITHS)
9 - JUST SOUTH OF MAP IS HIGH ST. KENSINGTON TUBE, COMMONWEALTH INSTITUTE, SLEAZY EARL'S COURT
10 - NORWEGIAN YWCA
11 - KENNING CAR RENTAL
12 - VERY CHEAP PHOTO COPY (USE YOUR HOTEL'S TRAVEL LIBRARY)

NOTE - BUSES 12 & 88 GO FROM HOLLAND PARK AVE & BAYSWATER ROAD TO OXFORD CIRCUS, PICADILLY, TRAFALGAR & WESTMINSTER.

mostly with Third World students is great if you want a truly world-wide dorm experience give them a call. 12 pounds in a shared room, including breakfast and a great dinner. Don't miss the 8:30 pm social hour with tea and cookies. Open to travelers only in July and August.

Norwegian YWCA (Norsk K.F.U.K.)—For women only (and men with Norwegian passports), this is an incredible value—lovely atmosphere, on quiet stately street, piano lounge, TV room, study, all rooms with private shower, all three meals included, single-11.50 pounds, double-10 pounds, triple-9 pounds, and 8 pounds each in quads. They have mostly quads so if you're willing to share with strangers you're most likely to get a place. Tel. 727-9897, 52 Holland Park, W11 3R5. (I wonder what's easier—getting a Norwegian passport or a sex change?)

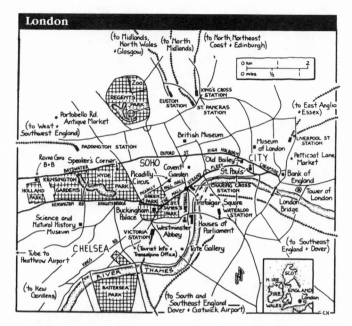

Catholic International Chaplaincy—Another gem, open to both men and women but only from mid-June to September 30, Father Maguire provides a TV lounge, study room, self-serve kitchen, garden, English breakfast and a very pleasant atmosphere for 8 pounds in a single or only 6 pounds in a double or triple. He will make reservations (10 pounds or $20 signed traveler's check deposit) for those staying for a week. Otherwise, call from the airport when you land. Tel. 727-3047, 41 Holland Park, W11 3RP.

Coleman Lodge Hotel—Big, hip, scruffy but comfortable, this was the best cheap hotel I found in the center. Student-oriented, bar, laundry, TV lounge, 8.50 pounds per person in double room with English breakfast. 31 Craven Hill Gardens, W2, Tel. 723-5988, near Lancaster Gate and Bayswater tube stations.

Youth Hostels—London has five or six official and more unofficial hostels. Personally, I'd stick to the official ones, but all are the large, impersonal, regimented big-city variety. They are very popular, always fill up, are equipped with good facilities, and are the cheapest beds in town—4 pounds.

Harlingford Hotel at 61 Cartwright Gardens, tel. 387-1551, is very well run and comfortable. Located near the British Museum (Russell Square tube) on a crescent with several other good budget B&B's, 28 pound doubles.

Holland Park Hotel—The most "hotellesque" of any of these places. Still, Roy and Joan Allen run this good value with a personal touch. 20 pounds single, 27 pounds double, 45 pounds triple, 55 pounds quad (more with private showers), TVs in each room, English breakfast, quiet, pleasant street, will accept telephone reservations without deposits if you'll arrive by mid-afternoon. 6 Ladbrook Terrace, W11 3PG, tel. 727-8166.

Near Victoria Station—Belgrave Road, Warwick Way and St. George Way are lined with reasonable B&B's.

Great Britain in 22 Days—Sample Itinerary

DAY 1 Arrive in London, visit the tourist information office to lay the groundwork for the next three weeks, get set up in your "bed and breakfast" and take an evening introductory walk through the heart of London.

DAY 2 Take the two-hour introductory double-decker bus tour of London before the 11:30 changing of the guard at Buckingham Palace. Then walk through the Piccadilly area to colorful Covent Gardens for lunch. Spend the afternoon touring the Tower of London with a Beefeater guide and take a close look at the crown jewels. Then take the Thames cruise from the bloody tower to Westminster, landing at the foot of Big Ben. Check out Westminster Abbey, possibly visit the Halls of Parliament to see the House of Commons in action, grab some pub grub for dinner and finish the day enjoying one of London's plays.

DAY 3 London has so much to see. Spend the morning touring the British Museum. After devouring Parthenon sculpture, Egyptian mummies, the Magna Carta and everything else in this attic of mankind, walk down Fleet Street for a pub lunch with London's harried newspaper crowd. Climb to the summit of St. Paul's, consider popping in to view the action at "Old Bailey," the high criminal court complete with powdered wigs and robes, or tour the London Stock Exchange before finishing your sightseeing day in the Museum of London.

DAY 4 Pick up your rental car at Heathrow airport to avoid crazy London driving, and drop by Salisbury to see its cathedral. Wander through the mysterious Stonehenge and Avebury stone circles before joy-riding through several picturesque villages and into Bath.

DAY 5 Tour Bath's Roman and Medieval mineral baths before a coffee break in the elegant Pump Room. Follow a local guide for two hours of history and highlights of England's trendsetting old world Hollywood. Spend the afternoon browsing and touring England's greatest collection of costumes—three hundred years of fashion history.

DAY 6 Today, sidetrip south exploring the haunted and entertaining Wookey Hole Caves, Wells with its medieval center and striking cathedral, and mystical Glastonbury—mythical home of Avalon, King Arthur and the Holy Grail. Evening free in Bath.

DAY 7 Drive into Wales, through its capital of Cardiff and to St. Fagan's Folk Museum—a park full of Welsh culture, restored old houses, and an intimate look at this fascinating culture. After a scenic drive up the Wye River Valley, past Tintern Abbey and through the Forest of Dean, set up at Stow-on-the-Wold in the heart of the Cotswold Hills.

DAY 8 Spend half the day savoring the most delicious of England's villages. This region is the quintessence of quaint. Then visit Blenheim Palace, Churchill's stately birthplace.

DAY 9 After a morning in Shakespeare's hometown, Stratford, tour England's finest medieval castle at Warwick and see the inspirational Coventry Cathedral—a charred ruin from the "blitz" with a shiny new church built more with love than with nails.

DAY 10 Today is devoted to the birthplace of the Industrial Revolution. The Ironbridge Gorge on the Severn River is a series of museums that take the visitor back into those heady days when Britain was racing into the modern age and pulling the rest of the West with her. Then it's into the romantic beauty of North Wales, setting up in Ruthin.

DAY 11 Circling scenic and historic North Wales, tour a woolen mill, the Caenarfon Castle, awesome Mount Snowdon and a bleak slate mine, arriving home in time to indulge in a medieval Welsh banquet—complete with harp, singing, pewter goblets of mead and daggers for meat-eating.

DAY 12 From the Garden of Eden to the garden of Hedon-ism: drive to Blackpool—England's Coney Island—for a look at the most popular tourist attraction in Britain that all Americans skip. Six miles of fortune tellers, fish 'n chips, amusement piers, beaches, warped mirrors and hordes of English. It's recess!

DAY 13 For another splash of contrast, drive into the pristine Lake District, inspiration for Wordsworth, with enough natural beauty to make anyone a poet. After a short cruise, and a six-

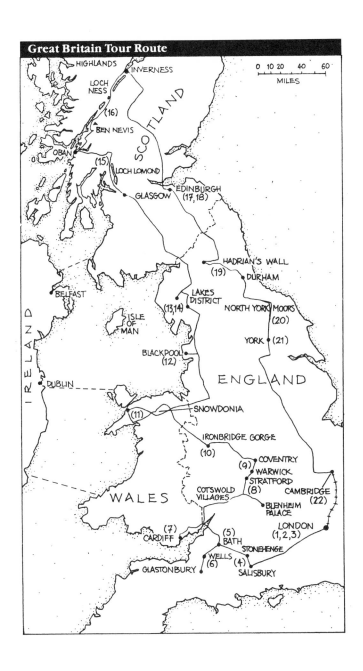

Great Britain Tour Route

mile walk around the loveliest of these lovely lakes, check into
a remote farmhouse bed and breakfast.

DAY 14 A pilgrimage to Wordsworth's famous Dove Cottage is
in order before enjoying a free day to relax, recharge, and take
the hike you like.

DAY 15 Now north into Scotland, past bustling Glasgow, along
the scenic Loch Lomond for a six hour drive to the Highlands.
Blaring bagpipes and swirling kilts accompany dinner tonight.

DAY 16 Today's all-day joy-ride features the stark beauty of
Glencoe, scene of a bloody clan massacre, a drive from coast to
coast along the Caladonian Canal and Loch Ness. Even if you
don't see the monster, you will tour a grand castle and enjoy
some fine Highland scenery. After a visit to Culloden, the site of
the last battle on British soil—and the end of Bonnie Prince
Charlie and Scottish hopes, you'll zip down from Inverness to
Edinburgh.

DAY 17 Edinburgh! one of Europe's most entertaining cities.
After a tourist office orientation, cover the Royal Mile, touring
the Edinburgh Castle, the Holyrood Palace—where the queen
stays when she's in town—and everything in between. This is
the colorful city of Robert Louis Stevenson, Walter Scott and
Robert Burns.

DAY 18 There's much more to see and do in Edinburgh: a con-
cert in the park, the elegantly Georgian new town, the best
shopping in Scotland, and an evening of folk music and dance.

DAY 19 Two hours south of Edinburgh, Hadrian's Wall reminds
us that Britain was an important Roman colony two thousand
years ago. After a walk along Hadrian's ramparts and through a
fine Roman museum, it's on to the fascinating Beamish Open
Air Museum for a look at life in the dawn of our century. Finally,
tour the Durham Cathedral, England's finest Norman church.

DAY 20 After a morning in the lonesome North York Moors
with its time-passed villages, bored sheep and powerful land-
scapes, set up in the city of York in time to enjoy an introductory walking tour by an old Yorker.

DAY 21 York has more than its share of blockbuster sights.
Divide this day between the great York Minster, the Jorvik
exhibit—the best Viking museum anywhere—and several

engrossing hours in the York Castle Museum—a walk with
Charles Dickens and the most eye-opening look at our past
you'll ever open your eyes for.

DAY 22 After a three-hour drive to Cambridge, check your
bags at the station, turn your car in, and spend the afternoon
exploring England's loveliest cluster of campuses. Cambridge,
with its sleepy river, lush green grounds, mellow study halls,
helpful tourist office and old streets clogged with bicycles, is
worth all the time you can muster today before catching the
hour long train ride into London.

The circle is complete and you've experienced the best 22 days
Britain has to offer. For 136 pages of step-by-step instructions
on this itinerary, use Rick's *Great Britain in 22 Days* (ISBN
0-912528-67-2, John Muir Publications, $5.95, 1987).

SPAIN & PORTUGAL

DAY 1 Fly to Madrid.

DAY 2 Arrive in Madrid, catch bus or taxi to Puerta del Sol to find your hotel. Get your bearings with an easy afternoon and evening. Possible stroll around old town.

DAY 3 Dive headlong into the grandeur of Spain's past, spending the morning at the lavish Royal Palace. After lunch and a siesta in the giant Retiro Park, cover the canvas highlights of the Prado museum and Picasso's Guernica.

DAY 4 Spend the morning browsing through Madrid's old quarter and maybe the huge flea market. The afternoon is free for a bullfight, a side trip to El Escorial, or shopping. Spend the evening in the busy Malasana quarter dining late like Spain does. (This day is one of 3 easy-to-cut days on this itinerary).

DAY 5 Pick up your rental car first thing this morning (or catch the train) and head for historic Segovia where you'll have four hours to tour its impressive Roman aqueduct, cathedral, and Alcazar fortress. After a few hours on the road, set up in Salamanca in time to join the "paseo" (city stroll) and linger over dinner on Spain's greatest square, the Plaza Mayor.

DAY 6 Spend the morning exploring the old town and Salamanca's venerable university. Drive for about an hour for lunch in the walled frontier town of Ciudad Rodrigo and then cross into Portugal, driving through its wildly natural countryside to Coimbra in time to find a hotel and enjoy a dinner in the old quarter.

DAY 7 Spend the morning enjoying the historic center of what was the Portuguese capital when the Moors held Lisbon. After touring the university—Portugal's Oxford—have lunch and drive south for two hours to Batalha, the country's greatest church and a 600 year old symbol of its independence from Spain. The fishing village of Sao Martinho is nearby. Find a room and enjoy dinner on the Atlantic coast.

DAY 8 There's plenty to do during a circular morning excursion to small towns. After visiting a wine museum and the Alcobaca monastery you'll be ready for lunch in Nazare—a fishing village turned Coney Island. The afternoon and evening are free to explore Nazare, soak up some sun, take a swim, sample today's

Spain and Portugal Tour Route

catch for dinner and watch the sun dive into the sea in Nazare or in our village homebase of Sao Martinho.

DAY 9 After breakfast, drive to Obidos—Portugal's medieval walled gem town—for a wander. Some of Portugal's most famous seafood is yours for lunch and you should be set up in Lisbon by 4:00. The salty Alfama quarter is a great place for an evening stroll and dinner.

DAY 10 This day in Lisbon is for relaxing, shopping and getting oriented. Spend the morning in the fashionable old Baixa and Chiado quarters shopping and people-watching. After lunch, enjoy the best view in town from the castelo and hike through the noisy nooks and cobbled crannies of the incredibly atmospheric Alfama sailors' district. Finish the day with drinking and droning in a gloomy Fado restaurant.

DAY 11 Now you get into Lisbon's history and art. The morning will be busy enjoying 2,000 exciting years of art in the

Gulbenkian Museum. After lunch, head out to the suburb of
Belem for a good look at the wonders of Portugal's Golden
Age—the huge Monument to the Discoveries, the Belem tower
and the great Manueline-style church and cloisters.

DAY 12 Today you make a circular trip from Lisbon. First to
Sintra with its hill-capping fairy-tale Pena Palace and the
mysterious and desolate ruined Moorish castle. Then on to the
wild and windy Capo da Roca. From this western-most point in
Europe, go to the stately resort town of Cascais for dinner and
an hour on the noble beachfront promenade.

DAY 13 Leave early for Evora, where you'll spend a few hours
exploring and having lunch. The afternoon will be spent driving
from remote village to village south through the vast Alentejo
region. By dinnertime you should be set up in your Algarve
hideaway—the tiny fishing village of Salema.

DAY 14 This is your "vacation from the vacation day," with
beach time and fun in the Algarve sun.

DAY 15 A day to explore Portugal's south coast. After an
elegant Pousada breakfast, drive to Cape Sagres, Europe's
"Land's End" and home of Henry the Navigator's famous
navigation school. Spend the afternoon and evening in the jet-
setty resort of Portimao or return to the peace and sleepy beauty
of Salema.

DAY 16 Leave early driving across the entire Algarve with a few
stops. By mid-afternoon you'll be on the tiny ferry, crossing the
river to Spain where you're just two hours from Sevilla.

DAY 17 Today is for exciting Sevilla. After a busy morning in
the Alcazar, Moorish garden, cathedral, climbing the Giralda
Tower and exploring the old Jewish quarter, you'll need a
peaceful lunch on the river and a siesta in the shady Maria
Louisa Park. Spend the late afternoon browsing through the
shopping district and visiting the Weeping Virgin altarpiece.
Sevilla is Spain's late-night capital—get swallowed up in the
ritual "paseo" and finish things off with dinner and a flamenco
show in the Santa Cruz neighborhood.

DAY 18 Leave Sevilla early and arrive in Ronda late, filling this
day with as much small town adventure as possible as you explore the "Ruta de Pueblos Blancos" —route of the white
villages. The Andalusian interior is dotted with friendly and
forgotten little white-washed towns.

DAY 19 After a morning to enjoy gorge-straddling Ronda's old town and bullring, leave the rugged interior for the famous beach resorts of the Costa del Sol. Spend half a day on the coast not to enjoy the beach and sun as much as to experience a social phenomenon—the devastation of a beautiful coastline by sun-worshipping human beings. The headquarters you choose will depend on the atmosphere you want—hip, aristocratic, package-tour-tacky or quiet.

DAY 20 Escape very early to arrive in Granada by 9:00 am. Spend most of the day in the great Moorish Alhambra palace with a picnic lunch in the royal Generalife gardens. Evenings are best spent exploring Spain's best old Moorish quarter, the Albaicin. This is a great place for dinner and an Alhambra view.

DAY 21 Drive all day to Toledo stopping for lunch in La Mancha, Don Quixote country. Get set up in the medieval depths of Toledo—Spain's best preserved and most historic city. An atmospheric (and delicious) roast suckling pig dinner is a great way to end the day.

DAY 22 Toledo has so much to see. Tour Spain's greatest cathedral and enjoy the greatest collections of El Greco paintings anywhere. Drive back to Madrid, turn in the car and check into the same hotel you stayed in when you began 22 days ago.

For a 136-page step-by-step guide to this itinerary, use Rick's *Spain & Portugal in 22 Days* (ISBN 0-912528-63-X, John Muir Publications, $5.95, 1987).

SCANDINAVIA

Sample 22-Day tour by car

DAY 1 Fly to Copenhagen.

DAY 2 Arrive at Copenhagen airport. Set up, orientation, relax.

DAY 3 Copenhagen city sights, palace, shopping, evening at Tivoli.

DAY 4 North Zealand, Frederiksborg Castle, Kronborg (Hamlet) Castle, Louisiana ultra-modern art museum, boats to Sweden. Evening in Lund.

DAY 5 Drive from Lund to Stockholm. Stockholm orientation.

DAY 6 Stockholm city sights—Gamla Stan, Royal Palace, historic center, smorgasbord midday feast, sauna.

DAY 7 Stockholm—Millesgarten, Wasa, Skansen Swedish Open-air Folk Museum. Evening fun at Skansen and Grona Lund amusement park.

DAY 8 Explore Uppsala—historic capitol and university town. Dalarna where the Swedish folk culture mixes so comfortably with the beautiful natural scenery.

DAY 9 Drive to Oslo, downtown sightseeing tour.

DAY 10 Oslo—city sights—boat to Bygdoy for open-air folk museum, Kon-Tiki, Ra, Fram and the best Viking ships anywhere.

DAY 11 Villages and Interior of Norway.

DAY 12 Interior and fjords of West Norway.

DAY 13 Bergen, historic and trading capitol.

DAY 14 Bergen, medieval stavechurch, Troldhaugen fjord country.

DAY 15 Fjord country, Setesdal Valley.

DAY 16 Setesdal—South Norway.

DAY 17 South Coast.

DAY 18 Boat to Jutland, Denmark.

DAY 19 Odense, Hans Christian Andersen Land.

DAY 20 Free day to be used anywhere on the tour.

DAY 21 Roskilde to Copenhagen.

DAY 22 Copenhagen, tour over, fly home when you like.

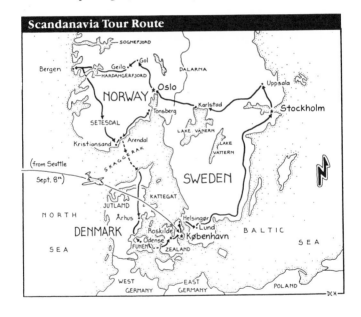

GREECE & YUGOSLAVIA

Sample tour by car

DAY 1 Fly USA-Athens. Hotel in Plaka.

DAY 2 Athens—Plaka, Agora, Acropolis, evening dine and dance in Plaka.

DAY 3 Athens—National Museum, pick up car, drive over Corinth Canal to Nafplion.

DAY 4 Nafplion—Morning, ruins of Mycenae; afternoon, Epidavros Theater; evening, seafood on Nafplion waterfront.

DAY 5 Nafplion—Sparta (lunch), Mystra—Byzantine ruins, Jerolimin—tiny coastal village.

DAY 6 Jerolimin—Pirgos Dirous caves—Koroni.

DAY 7 Koroni—Finikous, remote fishing village, great beach.

DAY 8 Finikous—drive north, explore Olympia ruins.

DAY 9 Long drive to Olympia—Rion ferry—Ionnina—Metsovo.

DAY 10 Metsovo—colorful Romanian town, good shopping. Meteora—pinnacle monasteries. Enchanting.

DAY 11 Meteora—Ohrid, Yugoslavia. Mysterious town on border of Albania. (*Sobe* means bed and breakfast in Yugoslavian.)

DAY 12 Ohrid—Prizren. This is a Muslim-Albanian world about as "un-western" as is possible in Europe.

DAY 13 Prizren—Pec. Make things happen here. The people are great.

DAY 14 Pec—Centinje, the historic capital of rugged Montenegro.

DAY 15 Centinje—Dubrovnik, stay in *sobe*. Don't miss the folk dancing at the Revelin Fort.

DAY 16 Dubrovnik. A free day for Europe's most romantic city.

DAY 17 Dubrovnik—Korcula. A mini-Dubrovnik on an island.

DAY 18 Korcula—Mostar—Sarajevo. A giant busy city with a fascinating old town.

DAY 19 Sarajevo—sightsee in the morning and drive through winding mountain roads to Titovo that evening.

DAY 20 Titovo—south by autobahn to any coastal town off freeway near Mt. Olympus.

DAY 21 Coastal town—Oracle of Delphi—sightsee ruins and museum.

DAY 22 Athens, turn in car.

DAY 23 Free day to plug in anywhere. A slack day is necessary in such a demanding car tour. Take freeways wherever possible but most of the driving will be slow, and unpredictable.

DAY 24 Fly home from Athens or sail to an island for more fun in the sun.

EUROPE ALMANAC

European Festivals

Each country has a "4th of July" celebration. A visit to a country during its national holiday can only make your stay more enjoyable.

Austria, October 26
France, July 14
Italy, June 2
Netherlands, April 30
Switzerland, August 1
West Germany, June 17

Netherlands

Kaasmarkt, Fridays only from late April to late Sept. Colorful cheese market with members of 350 year old Cheese Carriers' Guild. Alkmaar, 15 mi N of Amsterdam.

North Sea Jazz Festival, weekend of 3rd Sunday in July. World's greatest jazz weekend. 100 concerts with 500$ musicians. Den Haag.

Germany

Der Meistertrunk, Sat. before Whit Monday. Music, dancing, beer, sausage in Rothenberg ob der Tauber.

Pied Piper's Procession, Sundays, 1:00 p.m. all summer, Hamlin (where else?).

Ayinger Volkfest, 2nd thru 3rd weekend in June. White bear, concerts and Maypole dancing at Aying, 15 mi SE of Munich.

Freiburger Weinfest, last Fri. thru following Tuesday in June. Wine festival in Black Forest town of Freiburg.

Kinderzeche, weekend before 3rd Mon. in July to weekend after. Festival honoring children who saved town in 1640s. Dinkelsbuhl.

Trier Weinfest, Sat. to 1st Mon. in August. Trier.

Gaubondenfest, 2nd Fri. in Aug. for 10 days. Second only to Oktoberfest. Straubing, 25 mi SE of Regensburg.

Der Rhein in Flammen, 2nd Sat. in August. Dancing, wine and beer festivals, bonfires. Koblenz to Braubach.

Moselfest, last weekend in August or 1st in Sept. Mosel wine festival in Winningen.

Backfischfest, last Sat. in August for 15 days. Largest wine and folk festival on the Rhine in Worms.

Wurstmarkt, 2nd Sat. Sept. through following Tuesday, and 3rd Friday through following Monday. World's largest wine festival in Bad Durkheim, 25 mi. W. of Heidelberg.

Oktoberfest, starting 3rd to last Sat. in September through 1st Sun. in October. World's most famous beer festival, Munich.

Austria
Salzburg Festival, July 26-August 30. Greatest music festival, focus on Mozart.

Italy
Sagra del Pesche, 2nd Sunday in May. One of Italy's great popular events, huge feast of freshly caught fish, fried in world's largest pans. Camogli, 10 mi S of Genoa.
Festa de Ceri, May 15. One of the world's most famous folklore events, colorful pageant, giant feast afterwards. Gubbio, in hill country, 25 mi NE of Perugia.
"Palio of the Archers," last Sunday in May. Re-enactment of medieval crossbow contest with arms and costumes. Gubbio, 130 mi NE of Rome.
"Palio," July 2 and Aug 16. Horse race is Italy's most spectacular folklore event. Medieval procession beforehand. 35,000 spectators. Siena, 40 mi SW of Florence.
Joust of the Saracen, 1st Sunday in Sept. Costumed equestrian tournament dating from 13th century crusades against the Muslem Saracens. Arezzo, 40 mi SE of Florence.
Historical Regatta, 1st Sunday in Sept. Gala procession of decorated boats followed by double-oared gondola race. Venice.
Human Chess Game, 1st or 2nd weekend in Sept in even-numbered years. Medieval pageantry and splendor accompany re-enactment of human chess game in 1454. Basso Castle in Marostica, 40 mi NW of Venice.

Switzerland
Landsgemeinde, 1st Sunday in May. Largest open-air parliamentary session. Glarus, 40 mi SE of Zurich.
Montreux International Jazz Festival, 1st through 3rd weekends in July. Comprehensive annual musical events featuring top artists. Montreaux.
William Tell Plays, 2nd Thursday in July through 1st Sunday in Sept. Dramatic presentations retelling the story of William Tell. Open-air theatre. Interlaken.
Swiss National Day, August 1. Festive national holiday! Parades, concerts, bell ringing, fireworks, yodeling, boat rides. Nationwide.

France
Fetes de la St. Jean, around June 24. 3 days of folklore and bull running in streets. St. Jean de Luz (on coast, S of Bordeaux).
Tour de France, first 3 weeks of July, 2,000 mile bike race around France ending in Paris.

Maubeuge International Beer Festival, Thursday before July 14 for two weeks. Great entertainment and beer in largest beer tent. In Maubeuge near Belgian border.

Bastille Day, July 13 & 14. Great national holiday all over France. Paris has biggest festivities.

Great Festival of Corouaille, 4th Sunday in July. Huge Celtic folk festival at Quimper in Brittany.

Alsace Wine Fair, 2nd & 3rd weekends in August. Colmar.

Festival of Minstrels, 1st Sunday in Sept. Wine, music, folklore, etc. in Ribeauville, 35 mi S of Strasbourg.

Fete d'Humanite, 2nd or 3rd Sat. & Sun. of September. Huge communist fair. Colorful festivities—not all red. Paris.

England

Jousting Tournament of Knights, last Sun.& Mon. in May at Chilham Castle near Canterbury. Medieval pageantry, colorful.

Allington Castle Medieval Market, 2nd or 3rd Sat. in June in Maidstone (30 mi. SE of London). Medieval crafts and entertainment.

Druid Summer Solstice Ceremonies, June 20 or 21, Stonehenge. Hoods and white robes, rituals from midnight to sunrise at about 4:45 am.

Ainwick Medieval Fair, last Sun.in June to next Sat. Medieval costumes, competition, entertainment. Ainwick, 30 mi N of Newcastle.

Haslemere Early Music Festival, 2 Fridays before 4th Sat. in July. 16th-18th century music on original instruments. 40 mi S of London.

Sidmouth International Folklore Festival, 1st to 2nd Fridays in August, 300 events, 15 mi E of Exeter.

Reading Rock Festival, last weekend in August. England's best. 40 mi W of London.

Nottingham Goose Fair, 1st Thur.-Sat. in Oct. One of England's oldest and largest fairs. Nottingham.

Guy Fawkes Day, Nov. 5. Nationwide holiday.

European Weather

Here is a list of average temperatures and days of no rain. This can be helpful in planning your itinerary, but I have never found European weather to be particularly predictable.

(1st line, average daily low; 2nd line, ave. daily high; 3rd line, days of no rain).

	J	F	M	A	M	J	J	A	S	O	N	D
France	32°	34°	36°	41°	47°	52°	55°	55°	50°	44°	38°	33°
Paris	42°	45°	52°	60°	67°	73°	76°	75°	69°	59°	49°	43°
	16	15	16	16	18	19	19	19	19	17	15	14
Germany	29°	31°	35°	41°	48°	53°	56°	55°	51°	43°	36°	31°
Frankfurt	37°	42°	49°	58°	67°	72°	75°	74°	67°	56°	45°	39°
	22	19	22	21	22	21	21	21	21	22	21	20
Great Britain	35°	35°	37°	40°	45°	51°	55°	54°	51°	44°	39°	36°
London	44°	45°	51°	56°	63°	69°	73°	72°	67°	58°	49°	45°
	14	15	20	16	18°	19°	18	18	17	17	14	15
Italy	39°	39°	42°	46°	55°	60°	64°	64°	61°	53°	46°	41°
Rome	54°	56°	62°	68°	74°	82°	88°	88°	83°	73°	63°	56°
	23	17	26	24	25	28	29	28	24	22	22	22
Netherlands	34°	34°	37°	43°	50°	55°	59°	59°	56°	48°	41°	35°
Amsterdam	40°	41°	46°	52°	60°	65°	69°	68°	64°	56°	47°	41°
	12	13	18	16	19	18	17	17	15	13	11	12
SWITZERLAND	29°	30°	35°	41°	48°	55°	58°	57°	52°	44°	37°	31°
Geneva	39°	43°	51°	58°	66°	73°	77°	76°	69°	58°	47°	40°
	20	19	21	19	19	19	22	21	20	20	19	21

These are the train timetables for this proposed European tour. *Use these for planning only* to give you an idea of how many trains leave a day and how long the trips take. These times will change often. We cut out all the exceptions and "fine print" so don't use these for navigating. Confirm your departure plans at the train station's information desk upon arrival.

If you can't find your train trip listed, look for it in reverse order (from your destination to where you are) and assume the rides will be as common and as fast or slow.

⊠	Change trains	↝ Sleeping car.
ℝ	Seat reservation compulsory	⊣ Couchette car.
x	Weekdays, except public holidays	✕ Dining car or buffet car

Amsterdam to

London Victoria ↳

Ⓒ 6 59	14 36	⊠ Roosendaal
		⊠ Oostende ⇌ ⊠ Dover
Ⓓ 8 58	16 36	⊠ Roosendaal
		⊠ Oostende ⇌ ⊠ Dover
Ⓓ 9 32	19 17¹⁾	⊠ Hoek van Holland ↝
		⊠ Harwich
Ⓔ 11 56	19 06	⊠ Roosendaal
		⊠ Oostende ⇌ ⊠ Dover
Ⓢ 14 56	22 06	⊠ Roosendaal
		⊠ Oostende ⇌ ⊠ Dover
Ⓓ 20 31	8 58¹⁾	⊠ Hoek van Holland ↝
		⊠ Harwich

Ⓒ 1 VI–4 I, 21 III–30 V, except/sauf/ohne 25, 26 XII
Ⓓ except/sauf/ohne 25, 26 XII
Ⓔ 1 VI–3 XI, 10 XII–4 I, 25 III–30 V, except/sauf/ohne 24–26, 31 XII
¹⁾ London Liverpool Street

København

Ⓢ 8 02	19 09	
10 03	20 45	⊠ Osnabrück IC ✕
Ⓢ 20 03	8 09	⊣
Ⓦ 20 33	9 09	⊠ Amersfoort ⊣

Koblenz

6 59	10 37	TEE ✕
7 57	11 51	IC ✕
8 29	13 09	✕
8 56	12 57	IC ✕
9 49	13 51	⊠ Duisburg IC ✕
10 49	14 57	⊠ Duisburg IC ✕
12 49	16 51	⊠ Duisburg IC ✕
Ⓑ 14 49	18 51	⊠ Duisburg IC ✕
15 49	20 19	
17 15	21 39	
19 21	0 38	via Nijmegen
19 51	0 54	

Paris Nord

6 56	13 00	✕
Ⓒ 8 53	14 15	IC ✕
10 53	17 15	
12 26	18 56	⊠ Bruxelles Nord IC
Ⓓ 15 26	21 13	⊠ Bruxelles Midi IC ✕
15 54	22 06	✕
17 26	23 15	⊠ Bruxelles Midi
22 15	6 50	⊣

Ⓒ ①–⑥, except/sauf/ohne 14 VII, 20 IV
Ⓓ ①–⑤, ⑦, except/sauf/ohne 13 VII, 19 IV

Bern to

Genova

Ⓒ 7 21	13 35	
8 13	14 45	IC ⊠ Milano IC ✕
9 21	15 42	⊠ Milano
10 21	16 45	⊠ Brig IC ✕ ⊠ Milano IC ✕
13 21	19 42	⊠ Milano
15 21	21 42	⊠ Brig IC ⊠ Milano
17 21	23 42	⊠ Milano

Ⓒ 2 VI–18 X

Strasbourg

6 45	9 46	IC ⊠ Basel ✕
9 22	12 35	⊠ Olten IC ⊠ Basel
11 22	14 39	⊠ Olten IC ⊠ Basel ✕
13 45	17 02	⊠ Basel
14 45	17 51	IC¹⁾
15 45	19 36	⊠ Basel
Ⓑ 18 45	22 30	IC ⊠ Basel
21 45	1 55	⊠ Basel

¹⁾ Bern–Basel

Milano Centrale

6 21	10 55	⊠ Brig
8 13	12 25	IC
9 21	13 50	
10 21	14 50	⊠ Brig IC ✕
13 21	17 50	
15 21	19 50	⊠ Brig IC
17 21	21 45	

Paris Lyon

6 45	11 28	ℝ ⊠ Frasne TGV ✕
11 16	16 23	IC ✕ ⊠ Lausanne TGV ✕
16 52	21 31	ℝ ⊠ Frasne TGV ✕
18 16	23 26	IC ✕ ⊠ Lausanne TGV ✕
23 02	6 07	⊣

Roma Termini

6 21	16 48	⊠ Brig ⊠ Milano TEE ℝ ✕
8 13	18 40	IC ⊠ Milano Rapido ✕
9 21	22 30	⊠ Milano ✕
10 21	22 08	⊠ Brig IC ✕
		⊠ Milano TEE ℝ ✕
17 21	5 24¹⁾	⊠ Milano ↝ ⊣
20 21	7 58	↝ ⊣

¹⁾ Roma Tiburtina

Brussels to

Amsterdam CS

6 10	9 08
7 10	10 08
8 10	11 08
9 10	12 08
10 10	13 08
11 04	14 15
12 10	15 08
13 10	16 08
14 10	17 08
15 10	18 08
16 10	19 08
17 10	20 08
18 10	21 08
19 10	22 08
20 15	23 08
21 10	0 13

London Victoria

©	6 59	11 06	X Oostende ⇔ X Dover
D	8 13	15 06	X Oostende ⇔ X Dover
E	9 59	14 36	X Oostende ⇔ X Dover
©	12 05	16 23	X Oostende ⇔ X Dover
F	14 59	19 06	X Oostende ⇔ X Dover
G	16 59	0 05	X Oostende ⇔ X Dover
S	17 59	22 06	X Oostende ⇔ X Dover
S	23 41	7 06	X Oostende ⇔ X Dover

© except/sauf/ohne 25, 26 XII
D W, except/sauf/ohne 25 XII
E 1 VI–4 I, 21 III–30 V, except/sauf/ohne 25, 26 XII
F 1 VI–3 XI, 18 XII–4 I, 21 III–30 V, except/sauf/ohne 25, 26, 31 XII
G ①–⑥ 2 VI–26 IX

Paris Nord

	1 53	6 50	⊷
©	7 10	9 43	TEE ✕
	8 04	10 50	
	10 10	13 00	✕
©	11 49	14 15	IC ✕
	14 07	16 55	
	16 10	18 56	IC
D	17 14	19 44	TEE ✕
E	18 38	21 13	IC ✕
	19 12	22 06	✕
	20 41	23 15	

© ①–⑥, except/sauf/ohne 14 VII, 20 IV
D ①–⑥, ⑦ 1 VI–18 VII, 1 IX–29 V; ①–⑥ 21 VII–29 VIII, except/sauf/ohne 14 VII, 20 IV
E ①–⑤, ⑦, except/sauf/ohne 13 VII, 1 XI, 19 IV

Florence to

Pisa

6 00	6 48
7 05	8 00
7 45	8 49
9 00	9 54
9 40	10 35
11 00	11 54
12 00	12 54
13 00	13 54
14 00	14 54
15 00	15 54
16 00	16 54
17 00	17 54
18 00	18 54
19 00	19 54
20 50	21 45
22 42	23 12
23 35	0 59

Roma Termini

5 14	8 30	
7 00	10 15	
9 26	12 45	
10 15	14 38	
11 26	15 10¹)	
11 41	13 48	TEE R ✕
14 15	17 55	
15 24	17 40	R ✕
16 48	20 05	TEE R ✕
17 50	20 50	
18 50	22 30	
20 01	22 08	TEE R ✕
21 55	0 25	

¹) Roma Tiburtina

Venezia SL

1 38	5 37	⊷
6 25	10 26	
9 55	13 28	
11 35	15 15	
13 44	16 40	Rapido
14 20	18 15	
15 53	19 17	R ✕
16 43	20 24	
20 42	23 50¹)	

¹) Venezia Mestre

Venice to

Firenze

0 55	5 04	⊷ ⊷
5 28	9 30	✕
6 30	10 28	X Bologna
8 05	10 55	R ✕
10 25	14 05	✕
12 04	15 16	R ✕
12 50	16 23	X Bologna
14 00	18 40	X Bologna
15 35	19 52	X Bologna TEE R ✕
16 26	20 10	✕
17 00	20 50	
17 35	21 36	
18 30	23 20	X Bologna
20 55	0 42	

Roma Termini

0 55	8 30	⊷ ⊷
5 28	12 55	✕
8 05	13 48	R ✕ X Firenze TEE R ✕
10 25	17 55	✕
12 04	17 40	R ✕
12 50	18 40	X Bologna Rapido ✕
15 35	22 08	X Bologna TEE R ✕
16 26	22 54	✕
20 55	5 24¹)	X Bologna ⊷ ⊷
22 55	7 00	⊷ ⊷

¹) Roma Tiburtina

Frankfurt to

Amsterdam CS

4 37	11 14	⊠ Köln
6 48	12 14	⊠ Duisburg
7 26	13 14	
10 48	16 14	IC ✕ ⊠ Duisburg
Ⓐ 11 48	17 14	IC ✕ ⊠ Duisburg
12 48	18 14	IC ✕ ⊠ Duisburg
13 48	19 14	IC ✕ ⊠ Duisburg
14 46	19 59	IC ✕ ⊠ Duisburg IC ✕
15 46	20 59	IC ✕
Ⓑ 16 48	22 14	IC ✕ ⊠ Duisburg
18 48	0 21	IC ✕ ⊠ Duisburg

Berlin Zool. Garten

8 54	16 20	✕
9 24	17 09	IC ✕ ⊠ Hannover ✕
11 24	18 47	IC ✕ ⊠ Hannover ✕
13 24	20 38	IC ✕ ⊠ Hannover ✕
15 33	22 43	
22 35	6 13	⇌ ⊢

København

0 06	12 09	⇌ ⊢ ⊠ Hamburg
0 30	14 09	⇌ ⊢ ⊠ Hamburg
Ⓢ 8 23	19 29	IC ✕ ⊠ Hamburg
9 23	19 45	IC ✕ ⊠ Hamburg IC ✕
12 23	22 50	IC ✕ ⊠ Hamburg
16 31	6 45	⇌ ⊢

München
continued/suite/Fortsetzung

	13 24	IC ✕
9 21	14 03	IC ✕
Ⓒ 10 21	15 10	✕
10 50	15 24	IC ✕
11 21	16 03	IC ✕
12 21	17 03	IC ✕
13 21	18 27	IC ✕
14 21	19 03	IC ✕
15 21	20 24	IC ✕
16 21	21 05	IC ✕
Ⓑ 17 21	22 05	IC ✕
18 21	23 26	IC ✕
19 21	0 17	IC ✕ ⊠ Würzburg
Ⓑ 20 21		
Ⓒ ①–⑥		

Genoa to

Firenze

6 38	10 28	⊠ Pisa
8 11	12 26	✕ ⊠ Pisa
8 39	12 40	⊠ Pisa
10 08	13 25	ℝ ✕ ⊠ Pisa
12 07	15 40	✕ ⊠ Pisa
16 34	20 38	⊠ Pisa
20 02	23 30	⊠ Pisa

Nice

2 25	8 20	⊢
6 02	9 53	
8 23	11 18	IC ✕
16 02	19 16	
18 15	22 04	✕
20 02	23 40	

Roma Termini

0 15	7 00	⇌ ⊢
1 23	8 45	⇌ ⊢
6 38	13 56¹)	✕
8 11	13 55	✕
8 39	16 00	
10 08	15 30	ℝ ✕
12 07	17 45	
12 55	19 35	✕
16 34	22 52	
18 32	23 55	ℝ ✕
22 45	4 18¹)	⇌ ⊢
23 38	5 36¹)	⇌ ⊢

¹) Roma Ostiense

Innsbruck to

München

4 45	6 57
7 40	10 03
9 24	11 36
12 13	14 19 IC ✕
14 06	16 16
18 27	20 30
19 12	21 17

Strasbourg

4 45	12 21	⊠ München
	13 52	
Ⓒ 20 10	21 42	
	4 56	⊠ München ⇌ ⊢

Ⓒ Ⓢ: ⑥, ⑦

Venezia SL

0 55¹)	8 45	⊢
9 57	16 30	✕

¹) Ⓦ: dp/ab 1 42

London to

dp/ab London King's Cross

Edinburgh

Ⓒ 7 30	12 39	✕
Ⓒ 8 00	12 45	✕
⑦ 8 45	15 49	
Ⓒ 9 00	13 58	✕
⑥ 9 30	14 39	✕
⑦ 9 30	15 30	
Ⓒ 10 00	14 50	✕
Ⓒ 10 30	15 05	✕
Ⓒ 11 00	15 58	✕
⑦ 11 00	16 55	✕
Ⓒ 12 00	16 44	✕
⑦ 12 00	17 45	✕
Ⓒ 12 30	18 32	✕
Ⓒ 13 00	17 50	✕
Ⓒ 14 00	18 49	✕
⑦ 14 00	19 37	
Ⓒ 15 00	19 55	✕
⑦ 15 00	20 31	✕
16 00	20 45	✕
17 00	21 56	✕
18 00	23 03	✕
Ⓑ 23 35	8 00	only/seulement/nur ⊷

Ⓒ ①–⑧

dp/ab London Victoria

Oostende

8 15	12 45	⊠ Dover ⊊
9 15	16 00	⊠ Dover ⊷
11 30	16 00	⊠ Dover ⊊
13 10	20 00	⊠ Dover ⊊
13 30	18 05	⊠ Dover ⊊
16 00	20 30	⊠ Dover ⊊
19 00	23 30	⊠ Dover ⊊
Ⓒ 21 30	4 30	⊠ Dover ⊷

Ⓒ 1 VI–26 IX

dp/ab London Victoria

Amsterdam CS

8 15	17 36	⊠ Dover ⊊ ⊠ Oostende
		⊠ Roosendaal
9 15	20 36	⊠ Dover ⊷ ⊠ Oostende
		⊠ Roosendaal
⑦ 9 20¹⁾	21 32	⊠ Harwich ⊷
		⊠ Hoek van Holland
Ⓒ 9 40¹⁾	21 32	⊠ Harwich ⊷
		⊠ Hoek van Holland
11 30	20 36	⊠ Dover ⊊ ⊠ Oostende
		⊠ Roosendaal
13 30	22 36	⊠ Dover ⊊ ⊠ Oostende
		⊠ Roosendaal
19 50¹⁾	9 02	⊠ Harwich ⊷
		⊠ Hoek van Holland
Ⓓ 21 30	9 36	⊠ Dover ⊷ ⊠ Oostende
		⊠ Roosendaal

Ⓒ ①–⑧
Ⓓ 1 VI–26 IX
¹⁾ London Liverpool Street

dp/ab London Victoria

Paris Nord

8 04	18 07¹⁾	⊠ Newhaven ⊷ ⊠ Dieppe
Ⓒ 8 50	17 02	⊠ Dover ⊷ ⊠ Calais
9 45	17 50	⊠ Folkestone ⊷ ⊠ Boulogne
Ⓓ 10 55	21 02	⊠ Newhaven ⊷ ⊠ Dieppe
Ⓔ 10 55	21 15¹⁾	⊠ Newhaven ⊷ ⊠ Dieppe
11 10	19 20	⊠ Folkestone ⊷ ⊠ Boulogne
14 30	22 28	⊠ Dover ⊷ ⊠ Calais ✕
20 00	6 25¹⁾	⊠ Newhaven ⊷ ⊠ Dieppe
Ⓕ 22 55	9 15¹⁾	⊠ Newhaven ⊷ ⊠ Dieppe

Ⓒ ①–⑤, except/sauf/ohne 14 VII, 15 VIII
Ⓓ ①–⑧ 21 VI–6 IX, except/sauf/ohne 14 VII,
 15 VIII
Ⓔ ⑦ 22 VI–7 IX and/et/und 14 VII, 15 VIII
Ⓕ 27 VI–7 IX
¹⁾ Paris St-Lazare

Madrid to

dp/ab Madrid-Chamartin

Paris Austerlitz

8 10	23 24	⊠ Hendaye ✕
12 40	8 15	✕ ⊠ Hendaye
18 10	10 27	⊷ ⊶ ✕
19 40	8 48	ℝ ⊷ ✕
22 05	16 00	⊷ ⊶ ⊠ Hendaye ✕

Munich to

Frankfurt (Main)

Ⓒ 5 41	9 39	⊠ Würzburg IC ✕
6 35	10 38	IC ✕
Ⓒ 7 56	11 38	IC ✕
8 56	12 38	IC ✕
9 37	13 38	IC ✕
10 56	14 38	IC ✕
11 56	15 38	IC ✕
12 33	16 38	IC ✕
13 56	17 38	IC ✕
14 37	18 38	IC ✕
Ⓑ 15 56	19 38	IC ✕
16 37	20 38	IC ✕
Ⓑ 17 37	21 38	IC ✕ ⊠ Nürnberg IC ✕
18 37	22 39	IC ✕
Ⓑ 19 56	23 41	IC ✕

Ⓒ ①–⑥

Innsbruck

7 40	9 46	
8 20	10 25	ℝ ✕
13 33	15 44	ℝ
15 31	17 25	IC ✕
Ⓢ 17 17	19 14	IC ✕
19 20	21 30	ℝ
23 20	1 30	ℝ

Venezia SL

7 40	16 30	⊶
Ⓢ 22 36	8 45	⊶
Ⓦ 23 20	8 45	ℝ ⊶

Paris to

dp/ab Paris Nord — Amsterdam CS

© 7 10	13 06	TEE ✕ 🗵 Bruxelles Midi
7 48	14 15	
10 24	16 34	✕
© 11 35	17 06	IC 🗵 Bruxelles Midi
13 30	20 06	🗵 Bruxelles Midi
14 38	21 01	
16 44	22 44	
© 17 40	23 06	TEE ✕ 🗵 Bruxelles Midi
© 18 40	0 04	IC
23 15	8 01	⇥

© ①–⑥, except/sauf/ohne 14 VIII, 20 IV
© 1 VI–12 VII, 1 IX–30 V; ①–⑥, ⑦ 14 VII–31 VIII, except/sauf/ohne 19 IV
© ①–⑥, ⑦, except/sauf/ohne 13 VII, 31 XII, 19 IV

dp/ab Paris Nord — London Victoria [L]

© 0 20¹⁾	9 58	🗵 Dieppe ⛴ 🗵 Newhaven
© 7 55	13 53	🗵 Calais ⛴ 🗵 Dover
© 7 55	14 23	🗵 Calais ⛴ 🗵 Dover
© 9 20	13 40²⁾	🗵 Boulogne ⛴ 🗵 Dover
© 10 53¹⁾	18 39	🗵 Dieppe ⛴ 🗵 Newhaven
© 11 25	15 40²⁾	🗵 Boulogne ⛴ 🗵 Dover
© 12 30	18 36	🗵 Boulogne ⛴ 🗵 Folkestone
© 13 15	17 40²⁾	🗵 Boulogne ⛴ 🗵 Dover
© 14 20	18 40²⁾	🗵 Boulogne ⛴ 🗵 Dover
© 16 25	20 53²⁾	🗵 Boulogne ⛴ 🗵 Dover
© 17 04	23 06	🗵 Boulogne ⛴ 🗵 Folkestone
© 22 13¹⁾	6 43	🗵 Dieppe ⛴ 🗵 Newhaven

dp/ab Paris Austerlitz — Madrid-Chamartin

✕ 6 51	21 38	✕ 🗵 Irun IC ✕
14 24	8 52	✕ 🗵 Irun ⇥
17 45	10 00	⇥ 🗵 Hendaye IC
20 00	8 55	IC only/seulement/nur ⇥ ✕
22 15	17 33	⇥ 🗵 Irun ✕
22 40	16 05	only/seulement/nur ⛴ ⇥ 🗵 Irun IC ✕

Rome to

Firenze

7 00	9 46	
7 40	9 58	TEE ℝ ✕
8 25	11 12	✕
10 05	14 10	
11 35	13 43	TEE ℝ ✕
11 40	14 21	✕
13 25	15 45	ℝ ✕
14 00	16 28	Rapido
15 10	17 44	Rapido
17 05	19 37	Rapido
17 55	20 28	TEE ℝ ✕
19 45	22 05	Rapido
22 30	1 39	⇥

Genova

0 46¹⁾	7 17	⛴ ⇥
7 30	12 54	ℝ ✕
10 15	16 50	
12 08	17 55	
13 05	20 02	
14 00	19 26	ℝ ✕
15 45	21 33	✕
16 50	23 40	
18 45	23 45	ℝ ✕
22 00	4 51	⛴ ⇥
23 05	5 41	⛴ ⇥

¹) Roma Ostiense

Paris Lyon

0 58¹⁾	16 53	⛴ ⇥ 🗵 Milano IC
		🗵 Lausanne TGV ✕
7 40	21 31	TEE ℝ ✕ 🗵 Milano IC
		🗵 Lausanne TGV ✕
11 35	6 07	TEE ℝ ✕ 🗵 Milano ⛴ ⇥
15 45	8 55	⛴ ⇥
18 45	10 07	⛴ ⇥

¹) Roma Tiburtina

Salzburg to

München

5 12	7 03	
5 53	8 03	
7 08	9 18	
8 45	10 51	
9 20	10 59	
10 38	12 23	✕
11 56	13 32	✕
12 34	14 11	IC ✕
13 45	15 47	
14 47	16 55	
15 38	17 26	✕
16 13	18 26	
18 50	20 30	✕
20 47	22 41	
21 32	23 30	
Ⓢ 21 45	23 35	✕

Tours to

Paris Austerlitz

© 6 33	8 45	
Ⓐ 7 15	9 39	
7 55	9 57	🗵 St-Pierre-des-Corps ✕
© 8 54	11 24	
✕ 9 41	11 39	🗵 St-Pierre-des-Corps ✕
✕ 10 35	13 15	
11 55	13 46	🗵 St-Pierre-des-Corps IC ✕
✕ 13 13	15 33	
14 08	16 00	🗵 St-Pierre-des-Corps ✕
16 30	18 43	🗵 St-Pierre-des-Corps ✕
17 07	19 15	🗵 St-Pierre-des-Corps ✕
© 17 30	19 40	🗵 St-Pierre-des-Corps
✕ 18 15	20 30	
19 32	21 32	🗵 St-Pierre-des-Corps IC
20 56	23 12	🗵 St-Pierre-des-Corps
© 21 36	23 24	🗵 St-Pierre-des-Corps

© ①–⑥
© 28 VI–8 IX

Here are the schedules for the bus ride through the best of medieval Germany (about Frankfurt to Munich) and the boat ride past the best castles on the Rhine (Koblenz to Bingen). Both rides are included free with the Eurailpass. These connect at Weisbaden and give you the most interesting way to sightsee your way from Holland to Munich and Bavaria.

Romantic Road Bus Tour

V	W		Europabus 190		W	X
....	0815	dep.	*Frankfurt (Hbf.)* .... arr.		1955	....
0900	1015	dep.	**Würzburg** (Hbf.) .... arr.		1809	1920
1005	....	dep.	Bad Mergentheim .... dep.		|	1815
1200	1135	arr.⎫	Rothenburg/*Tauber*	⎰dep.	1700	1700
1330	1345	dep.⎭		⎱arr.	1515	1535
1415	1430	dep.	Feuchtwangen .... dep.		1430	1455
1430	1445	arr.⎫	Dinkelsbühl	⎰dep.	1415	1440
1500	1530	dep.⎭		⎱arr.	1235	1310
1525	1605	dep.	Nördlingen .... dep.		1155	1230
1610	1635	dep.	Donauwörth .... dep.		1105	1200
1705	1735	arr.⎫	**Augsburg** (Hbf.)	⎰dep.	1020	1110
1715	1740	dep.⎭		⎱arr.	1010	1100
1935	....	arr.	**Füssen** (Postamt) .... dep.		|	0815
....	1855	arr.	*München (Hbf.)*		0900	....

V		Europabus 189		V
....	0715 .... dep.	Mannheim (Hbf.) .... arr.	.... 2045	
....	0745 .... dep.	Heidelberg (Hbf.) .... arr.	.... 2025	
....	1200 .... arr.	Rothenburg/Tauber .... dep.	.... 1650	

V— Daily, June 2–Sept. 28.   **W**—Daily, March 16–Nov. 4.   **X**— Daily, June 2–Sept. 29.

Rhine Cruise

SUMMER SERVICE ONLY: APRIL 4–OCTOBER 28 (NO SERVICE IN WINTER)
For the through services Rotterdam–Mannheim–Basel and v.v. see Table 366.

One class only.

m.v. Berlin.   m.v. Drachenfels.   p.s. Goethe.   m.v. Stolzenfels.
m.v. Bonn.   m.v. Düsseldorf.   m.v. Koblenz.   m.v. Trier.
m.v. Deutsches Eck.   m.v. Frankfurt.   m.v. Köln.   m.v. Rheingold.   m.v. Wiesbaden.
            m.v. Loreley.   p.s. Rüdesheim.
A reduced service operates on July 6 and Aug. 10.

Tar. km			S	D	Exp O	N	U	X	E	H	P	fast C5	A	V	G	C	Q	F	H	J	M	B
						1100			1120	1335	1355		1395				1545		1710		1900	....
100	Koblenz	arr.				1105			1130	1130	1340	1400	1400		1400	1430					1903	....
		dep.		0900	0924				1155	1155					1425	1455						....
106	Niederlahnstein	dep.		0924						1155			d		1455	1525					1950	....
112	Braubach	dep.		0958				1250	1315	1315					1525	1545	1615				2030	....
121	Boppard	dep.		0900	1040	1130				1430	1430				1655	1725						....
127	St. Goarshausen	dep.		1010	1150		1330	1330	1400	1630	1630			1705	1735							....
137	St. Goar	dep.		1015	1155	1150	1340	1340	1405	1440	1440			1725	1725							....
154	Bacharach	dep.		1120	1255	1208	1445	1445	1505	1545	1545			1810	1840							....
166	Assmannshausen	dep.		1225	1350		1536	1540	1600	1640	1640			1810	1810	1905	1935						....
170	Bingen	dep.		1256	1420		1228	1602	1610	1630	1710	1710			1835	1835	1930	2000					....
172	Rüdesheim	arr.		1310	1430		1233	1620	1620	1640	1720	1720			1850	1850	1940	2010					....
187	Eltville	dep.						1725	1745	1825	1825			1955	1955								....
195	Wiesbaden-Biebrich	arr.				1300	1800	1810	1835	1910	1910			2040	2040								....
200	Mainz	arr.				1310	1819	1830	1855	1930	1930			2100	2100								....
225	Frankfurt/Main	arr.					2130e																....

Tar. km			R	fast L4	L	X	J		F		B	N	U	Y	E	T	E		Exp P O	J	K
25	Frankfurt/Main	dep.									0715e											
25	Mainz	dep.		0845	0845					1015	1015			1045					1425			
5	Wiesbaden-Biebrich	dep.		0905	0905					1035	1035			1105					1433			
13	Eltville	dep.		0925	0925						1055			1125								
28	Rüdesheim	dep.		1025	1035	0950	0950			1145	1145			1220	1400	1400			1500	1600	1620	
30	Bingen	dep.		1045	1045	1010	1010			1200	1200			1235	1415	1415			1505	1605	1620	
34	Assmannshausen	dep.		1100	1100	1025	1025			1215	1215			1250	1430	1430				1615	1640	
48	Bacharach	dep.		1130	1130	1055	1055			1240	1240			1325	1505	1505				1650	1720	
63	St. Goar	dep.		1200	1200	1135	1135					1310	1320		1410	1550	1550				1730	1800	
63	St. Goarshausen	dep.		1210	1210	1145	1145					1315	1325		1420	1600	1600				1730	1810	
72	Boppard	dep.		1250	1250	1235	1235							1510	1645	1645		d	1555	1820	1850	
88	Braubach	dep.		1315	1315	1305								1540	1715	1715					1850	1920	
95	Niederlahnstein	dep.				1330								1602	1717	1737					1912	1942	
100	Koblenz	arr.		1345	1345	1350								1620	1755	1755		1700	1618	1930	2000	
		dep.			1405										1550	1800			1705	1620			

A— Daily, Apr. 4–30.	**P**— Mons., June 17–Sept. 30, also Tues. and Thurs. July 2–Aug. 9.
B— Suns., May 5–June 9.	**Q**— Sats. and Suns., June 29–Aug. 11.
C— Daily, May 1–Sept. 16.	**R**— Daily, Apr. 5–30 and Oct. 8–20 (also Rüdesheim–Koblenz, Oct. 21–28).
D— Daily, April 5–Oct. 27.	**S**— Daily, June 5–Sept. 16.
E— Daily, June 16–Sept. 16.	**T**— Daily, Sept. 17–29.
F— Daily, April 20–Sept. 16, also Apr. 6, 7, 13, 14.	**U**— Daily, Sept. 15.
G— Daily, Sept. 17–Oct. 27.	**V**— Daily except Mons., Sept. 17–29.
H— Daily, June 5–Sept. 16.	**W**— Daily, May 12–Oct. 5.
J— Daily, Oct. 8–27.	**X**— Daily, Oct. 9–20.
K— Daily, April 5–Oct. 7.	**Y**— Daily except Mons., Sept. 17–29, also Sats. and Suns., June 29–Aug. 11.
L— Daily, May 1–Sept. 16 (not Andernach–Boppard on Sats.).	**d**— Daily except Fris., June 16–Sept. 16 (also May 4, 5, 11, 12).
M— Daily, May 1–June 15; daily except Fris., June 16–Sept. 16.	**e**— Rhine/Moselle excursions to/from Kobern (Moselle).
N— Daily, June 16–Sept. 16.	**●**— 10 mins. later, Sept. 17–Oct. 7.
O— Express service, daily except Mons., May 1–Oct. 20 by hydrofoil *Rheinpfeil*. Also runs Sats. and Suns., Apr. 6–28 and Oct. 25–27. Special fares apply.	**1**— Fast ship, supplement payable (not applicable between Koblenz and Köln Sept. 17–Oct. 7).
	2— Fast ship, supplement applicable only from Koblenz to Mainz.

Telephone Directory

City	Long Distance Telephone Codes	Tourist Info
Amsterdam	020	266444
Delft	015	
St. Goar (Rhine)	06741	
Rothenburg	09861	2038
Munich	089	2391259
Reutte (Tyrol)	05672	
Innsbruck	05222	25715
Venice	041	715016, 700792, 27402 (rooms)
Florence	055	216544, 2468141, 282893 (rooms)
Orvieto	0763	6984466
Vatican	06	
Rome	06	4750078, 463748, 4740856 (rooms)
La Spezia (Cinqueterre)	0187	36000
Monterosso (Cinqueterre)	0187	817506
Interlaken (Jungfrau)	036	222121
Grindelwald	036	531212
Lauterbrunnen	036	551955
Colmar (Alsace)	089	416680
Reims	026	472569
Paris	01	47208898 (taped), 47236172, 45269482, 46071773, 45849170
London	01	730-3488

Schiphol Airport (Amsterdam) flight info:

charters	5110666
regular flights	5110432

Paris train info, north
and to Britain   42800303

Country Prefix Codes:

Netherlands	31
Belgium	32
Germany	49
Austria	43
Italy	39
Switzerland	41
France	33
England	44

Direct dial international telephoning is very important to do this 22-day plan smoothly. Coin-op international phone booths abound. To dial international, you dial: 1st—international access code, normally listed on booth; 2nd—country code; 3rd—the area code without the zero; 4th—the local number. To make the same call long distance from within the country, start with the area code including the zero. Booths normally have a toll-free English-speaking long distance information number posted. Phone info in English is often in the first pages of the telephone directory.

Foreign Money

Netherlands
Guilders (fl) divided into 100 cents (c)
1 guilder = about 40 cents
1 dollar = about 2.5 fl (guilders)
(multiply by four and divide by ten to get dollars. E.g., 15 fl = $6)
Exact exchange rate _____

Germany
Deutsch Marks (DM) divided into 100 pfennige (p)
1 DM = about 50 cents
1 dollar = about 2 DM
1 DM = about 1 fl
Exact exchange rate _____

Austria
Schilling (S or AS) dividied into 100 groschen (g)
1 S = about 6.5 cents
1 dollar = about 15 S
7 S = about 1 DM
Exact exchange rate _____

Italy
Lire (*L*)-One lire is a miniscule amount, so we'll work with units of 1000.
1 dollar = about 1500 *L*
Exact exchange rate _____ *L* = $1

Switzerland
Swiss Franc (SF or F) divided into 100 rappen (rp) or centimes (c)
1 SF = about 60 cents
1 dollar = about 1.7 SF
Exact exchange rate _____

France
Franc (F) divided into 100 centimes (c)
1 F = about 14 cents
1 dollar = about 7 F
Exact exchange rate _____

England
Pound divided into 100 pence
1 pound = about $1.50
1 dollar = about 70 pence
Exact exchange rate _____

Youth Hostels

Youth hosteling is the cheapest way to travel. Europe's 2,000 hostels, charging $4-6 per night, provide kitchens for self-cooked meals. They have curfews (generally 11:00), mid-day lock-ups (usually 9:00-5:00), require sheets (you can rent one), membership cards ($20 per year from your local USA office) and, except for southern Germany, are open to "youths" from 8 to 80. Here are the hostels lying along the part of our 22-day route:

Netherlands

Amsterdam—Stadsoelen, Kloveniersburgwal 97, 1011 KB Amsterdam; 184 beds; Metro: Niewmarkt; bus 4, 5, 9, 16, 24, 25; tel. 020/246832.

Vondelpark, Zandpad 5, Vondelpark, Vondelpark, 1054 GA Amsterdam; 300 beds; bus 1, 2, 3, 6, 7, 10; tel. 020/831744.

Haarlem—Jan Gijzenpad 3, 2024 CL Haarlem-Noord; 108 beds; 3km bus 2, 6; tel. 023/373793.

Germany (Jugendherberge)

Bacharach—Jugendburg Stahleck, 6533 Bacharach/Rhein; 207 beds; tel. 06743/1266. Wonderful castle hostel, 15 minutes above town, view of Rhine.

Bingen-Bingerbruck —Herter Str. 51, 6530 Bingen 1-Bingerbruck/Rhein; 194 beds; tel. 06721/42163.

Oberammergau —Malensteinweg 10, 8103 Oberammergau; 130 beds; tel. 08822/4114.

Oberwesel —Jugendgastehaus, Auf dem Schonberg, 6532 Oberwesel; 102 beds; tel. 06744/8355.

St. Goar —Bismarckweg 17, 5401 St Goar; 160 beds; tel. 06741/388.

Rothenburg/Tauber—Rossmuhle 8803 Rothenburg/Tauber; 141 beds; tel. 09861/4510.

Spitalhof, Postfach 1206, 8803 Rothenburg/Tauber; 90 beds; tel. 09861/7889.

Creglingen —Erdbacherstr. 30, 6993 Creglingen; 114 beds; tel. 07933/336.

Dinkelsbuhl —Koppengasse 10, 8804 Dinkelsbuhl; Open March 1 - Oct 31; 150 beds; tel. 09851/509.

Munchen —Wendl-Dietrich Str. 20, 800 Munchen 19; trolley 21, Rotkreuzplatz; tel. 089/131156.

Jugendgastehaus, Miesingstr. 4, 8000 Munchen 70; trolley 16, 26, Boschetsrieder Str.; tel. 089/7236550.

Pullach—Munich, Burg Schwaneck, Burgweg 4-6, 8023 Pullach; 130 beds; tel. 089/7932381. (A renovated castle.)

Fussen —Mariahilferstr. 5, 8958 Fussen; 150 beds; tel. 08362/7754.

Garmisch-Partenkirchen —Jochstr. 10, 8100 Garmisch-Partenkirchen; 290 beds; tel. 08821/2980.

Austria (Jugendherberge)
Reutte —6600 Reutte, Prof. Dengel-Strasse 20, Tirol; 28 beds; tel. 05672/3039.
Reutte-Hofen —6600 Reutte, Jugengastehaus am Graben, Postfach 3, Tirol; 38 beds; tel. 05672/2644,860.
Innsbruck —6020 Innsbruck, Reichenauerstrasse 147, Tirol; 190 beds; tel. 05222/46179.
    Studentenheim, 6020 Innsbruck, Reichenauerstrasse 147; 112 beds; tel. 05222/46179.
    6020 Innsbruck, Rennweg 17b, Tirol; 100 beds; tel. 05222/25814.
    6020 Innsbruck, Sillg. 8a, Tirol; 100 beds; 05222/31311.
    6020 Innsbruck, Volkshaus, Radetzkystr. 47; 52 beds; 05222/466684.

Italy (Ostello)
Siena —"Guido Riccio," Via Fiorentina (Lo Stellino), 53100 Siena; 110 beds; tel. (0577)52212.
Venezia —Fondamenta Zitelle 86, Isola della Giudecca, 30123 Venezia; 320 beds; tel. 041/38211.
Arezzo —Via Borg'Unto 6, 52100 Arezzo; 40 beds; tel. 0575/354546.
Cortona —Via Maffei 57, 52044 Cortona; 80 beds; tel. 0575/601392.
Firenze —Viale Augusto Righi 2-4, 50137 Firenze; 400 beds; tel. 055/601451.
    Ostello Santa Monaca, via Santa Monaca 6, Firenze 26-83-38. (unofficial, no card required.)
Lucca —"Il Serchio," Via del Brennero (Salicchi), 55100 Lucca; 90 beds; tel. 0583/953686.
Roma —"Aldo Franco Pessina," Viale delle Olimpiadi 61 (Foro Italico), 00194 Roma; 350 beds; tel. 06/3964709.

Switzerland (Jugendherberge/Auberge de Jeunesse/Ostello)
Gimmelwald-Murren —Beim Rest Schilthorn, 3801 Gimmelwald; 44 beds; tel. 036/551704.
Grindelwald —Terrassenweg, 3818 Grindelwald; 133 beds; tel. 036/531009.
Interlaken-Bonigen—Aareweg 21, am See, 3806 Bonigen; 200 beds; tel. 036/224353.

France (Auberge de Jeunesse)
Colmar—7 rue St Niklaas, 68000 Colmar (Haut-Rhin); 65 beds;
tel. 89/413308.
Paris—8 Boulevard Jules Ferry, 75011 Paris; 99 beds; tel.
1/3575560.
  Choisy-le-Roi, 125 Avenue de Villeneuve-St-Georges, 94600
Choisy-le-Roi; 280 beds; tel. (16) 1/8909230.
  Rueil-Malmaison, 4 rue des Marguerites, 92500 Rueil-
Malmaison; 96 beds; tel. 1/7494397.

DUTCH

Hello   Goedemiddag
Goo-der-mid-dahkh
Goodbye   Tot ziens
Tot seenss
Please   Alstublieft
Ahls-stew-bleeft
Thank you   Dank u
Dahngk ew
One   Een
Any
Two   Twee
Tvay
Three   Drie
Dree
Four   Vier
Veer
Five   Vijf
Vayf
Six   Zes
Zehss
Seven   Zeven
Zay-vern
Eight   Acht
Ahkht
Nine   Negen
Nay-gern
Ten   Tien
Teen
Twenty   Twintig
Tvin-tich
Fifty   Vijftig
Vayf-tich
One Hundred   Honderd
Hon-derrt
Yes   Ja
Yar
No   Nee
Nay
Cheap/Expensive   Goedkoop/Duur
Goot-koap/Dewr
Cheers   Proost!
Proast!

Beautiful   Mooi
Moaee
Delicious   Uitstekende
Oit-stay-kun-duh
What do you call this?   Hoe noemt u dat?
Hoo noomt ew daht?
I don't understand.   Ik begrijp het niet.
Ik ber-grayp-heht neet.
How are you?   Hoe gaat het?
Hoo gart hurt?
Excuse me   Neemt u me niet kwalijk
Naymt ew mer neet kvar-lerk
Very   Zeer
Zayr
Good/Bad   Goes/Slecht
Goot/Slehkht
Big/Small   Groot/Klein
Groat/Klayn
Fast/Slow   Snel/Langzaam
Snehl/Lahng-zarm
Where is. . .?   Waar is. . .?
Wahr is. . .?
How much?   Hoeveel
Hoo vill?
Friend   Vriend
vrent
Toilet   w.c.
vay say
Water   Water

GERMAN

Hello   Guten tag
Goo-ten tock
Goodbye   Auf wiedersehn
awf VEE-der-sayn
See you later   Bis spater
bees SHPAY-tuh
Goodnight   Gute nacht
GOO-tuh nahkt
Please   Bitte
BIT-teh
Thank you   Danke schon
DONG-kuh shayn
Yes/No   Ja/Nein
Yah/Nine
One/Two/Three   Eins/Zwei/Drei
Aintz/Tsvy/Dry
Cheap/Expensive   Billig/Teuer
BIL-ikh/TOY-err
Good/Bad   Gut/Schlecht
Goot/Shlehkht
Beautiful/Ugly   Schon/Hasslich
Shurn/HESS-leek
Big/Small   Gross/Klein
Groass/Kline
Fast/Slow   Schnell/Langsam
Shnel/LONG-zahm
Very   Sehr
Zair
Where is . . .?   Wo ist . . .?
Vo ist . . .?
How much?   Wieviel?
Vee-FEEL?
I don't understand.   Ich verstehe nicht.
Ikh ver-SHTAY-er nicht
What do you call this?   Wie heisst das?
Vee HEIST dahss?
I'm lost.   Ich habe mich verirrt.
Ikh hah-beh mikh fer-IRT
Complete price (everything included)   Alles ist
inbegriffen
AH-lerss ist IN-ber-grif-ern
I'm tired.   Ich bin mude.
Ikh bin MEW-duh

I'm hungry.   Ich habe hunger.
Ikh hah-beh HOONG-guh
Cheers!   Prosit!
Proast!
Food   Speise
SHPY-zuh
Grocery store   Laden
LODD-en
Picnic   Picknick
Pik-nik
Delicious   Lecker
LECK-uh
Market   Markt
Markt
Drunk   Betrunken
Beh-TROHN-ken
Money   Geld
Gelt
Station   Bahnhoff
BAHN-hof
Private accommodations   Zimmer
TSIMM-er
Toilet   Klo
Kloh
I   Ich
Eekh
You   Du
Doo
Love   Liebe
LEE-beh
Sleep   Schlaf
Shloff
Train   Zug
Tsoog
The bill, please.   Die rechnung, bitte.
Dee RECK-nung, BIT-teh.
Friend   Freund
Froint
Water   Wasser
VOSS-ehr
Castle   Schloss
Shlohss
How are you?   Wie geht es?
Vee GATES?
I'm fine, thanks.   Es geht mir gut, danke.
Es GATE mehr GOOT, DONG-kuh.
Tourist Information   Reiseburo
RIE-suhByoo-ro

ITALIAN

Hello   Buongiorno
Bohn-ZHOOR-no
Goodbye   Ciao
Chow
See you later   Civediamo
Chee-vey-dee-OMM-o
Good night   Buonna notte
BWONN-ah NOT-tay
Please   Per favore
Pair fah-VOR-ay
Thank you   Grazie
GRAH-tsee-ay
Yes/No   Si/No
See/NO
One/Two/Three   Uno/Due/Tre
Oo-noh/Doo-ay/Tray
Cheap/Expensive   Economico/Caro
Ay-koh-NO-mee-koh/CARR-o
Good/Bad   Buono/Cattivo
BWON-o/Kaht-TEE-vo
Beautiful/Ugly   Bello/Brutto
BEHL-lo /BROOT-to
Big/Small   Grande/Piccolo
GRAHN-day/PEEK-koh-lo
Fast/Slow   Rapido/Lento
RAHH-pee-do/LEHN-to
Very   Molto
MOHL-to
Where is. . .?   Dove. . .?
do-VAY. . .?
How much?   Quanto?
KWAHN-to?
I don't understand.   Non capisco.
Nohn kay-PEESS-ko.
What do you call this?   Che cosi quiesto?
kay KO-see KWAY-sto?
I'm lost.   Mi sono perso.
Mee SOH-no PEHR-so.
I'm tired.   Sono stanco.
SOH-no STAHNG-ko.
I'm hungry.   Ho fame.
Oh FAH-may
Food   Cibo
CHEE-bo

Grocery store   Drogheria
Dro-GAY-ree-ah
Picnic   Picnic
Picnic
Delicious   Delizioso
Day-leet-see-OH-so
Market   Mercato
Mayr-COT-to
Drunk   Ubriaco
Oo-bree-AH-co
Money   Denaro
Day-NAHR-ro
Station   Stazione
STAHT-see-OH-nay
Private accommodations   Camera
CAH-may-rah
Toilet   Toilet
Toy-LET
I   Io
ee-OH
You   Lei
Lay
Sleep   Dormire
Dor-MEER-ay
Train   Treno
TREN-no
The bill, please.   Il conto, prego.
Ell KON-to, pray-go.
Friend   Amico
Ah-mee-ko
Water/Tap water   Acqua/Acqua naturale
AH-kwa/AH-kwa nah-toor-ALL-ay
Castle   Castello
Kah-STELL-o
Church   Chiesa
Kee-AY-za
How are you?   Come va?
KO-may VAY?
Tourist Information   Ufficio informazioni
Oo-FEE-see-o EEN-for-MOTZ-ee-OH-nee
You're welcome   Prego
PRAY-go
Doing sweet nothing   Dolce far niente
DOL-chay far nee-YEN-tay

FRENCH

Hello   Bonjour
Bohn-ZHOOR
Goodbye   Au revoir
Oh-VWAH
See you later   A bientot
Ah byuhn-TOH
Good night   Bonne nuit
Bohn NWEE
Please   S'il vous plait
See voo PLAY
Thank you   Merci
Mehr-SEE
Yes/No   Oui/Non
Wee/Noh
One/Two/Three   Un/Deux/Trois
Uh/Doo/Twah
Cheap/Expensive   Bon marche/Cher
Bohn mar-shay/Shehr
Good/Bad   Bon/Mauvais
Bohn/Mo-VAY
Beautiful/Ugly   Joli/Laid
Zho-LEE/Lay
Big/Small   Grand/Petit
Grahn/Peh-TEE
Fast/Slow   Rapide/Lent
Ra-PEED/Lehn
Very   Tres
Tray
Where is. . .?   Ou est. . .?
Oo ay. . .?
How much?   Combien?
Kohm-bee-UHN
I don't understand.   Je ne comprends pas.
Zhuh neh COHM-prahn PAH
What do you call this?   Qu'est-ce que c'est?
KESS koo SAY
I'm lost.   Je me suis perdu.
Zhuh mah swee pehr-DOO
Complete price (everything included)   Tout est compris
Too-tay kohm-PREE
I'm tired.   Je suis fatigue.
Zhuh swee fah-tee-GAY
I'm hungry.   J'ai faim.
Zhay fam

Cheers!   Sante!
Sahn-TAY
Food   Nourriture
New-ree-TOOR
Grocery store   Epicerie
Eh-PEES-eh-REE
Picnic   Pique-nique
Peek-neek
Delicious   Delicieux
De-lee-syoh
Market   Marche
Mar-SHAY
Drunk   Soul
SOO
Money   Argent
Ar-ZHA
Station   Gare
Gar
Private accommodations   Chambre
Shambr
Toilet   w.c.
VAY-say
I   Je
Zhuh
You   Vous
Voo
Love   Amour
Ah-MOOR
Sleep   Sommiel
So-MAY
Train   Train
Tran
The bill, please.   L'addition, s'il vous plait.
Lah-dee-see-OHN, see voo play
Friend   Ami
Ah-MEE
Water/Tap water   Eau/Eau douce
Oh/OH doos
Castle   Chateau
Shat-TOH
How are you?   Ca va?
Sah VAH?
I'm fine.   Ca va.
Sah VAH
Tourist information   Syndicat d'initiative
San-dee-KAH dan-EE-see-ah-TEEV

BACK DOOR CATALOG

ALL ITEMS FIELD TESTED, HIGHLY RECOMMENDED, COMPLETELY
GUARANTEED AND DISCOUNTED BELOW RETAIL.

Back Door Combination Ruck Sack / Suitcase $60

At 9" × 21" × 13", this specially designed, sturdy functional bag is maximum carry-on-the-plane size. (Fits under the seat.) Constructed by Jesse Ltd. of rugged waterproof nylon Cordura material, with hide-away shoulder straps, waist belt (for use as a ruck sack) and top and side handles and a detachable shoulder strap (for toting as a suitcase). Perimeter zippers allow easy access to the roomy (2200 cu. in.) central compartment. Two small outside pockets are perfect for maps and other frequently used items. Two thousand Back Door Travelers took these bags around the world last year and returned satisfied. Comparable bags cost much more. If you're looking for maximum "carry-on size" and a suitcase that can be converted into a back pack, this is your best bet. Available in navy blue, black, gray, or burgundy.

Money belt $6.00

Required! Ultra-light, sturdy, under-the-pants, nylon pouch just big enough to carry the essentials comfortably. I'll never travel without one and I hope you won't either. Beige, nylon zipper, one size fits all, with instructions.

Sturdy Day Rucksack $8.00

This lightweight, 8" × 16" × 4" blue nylon bag is ideal for day-tripping. Leave your suitcase in the hotel, on the bus, or at the station, and run around with this on your back. Folds into its own pocket.

Globetrotting $6.00

by Rick Steves (1985, 250 pp., retail $7.95)

A collection of 60 completely new Back Doors in Europe, Asia and the Americas. Over 250 fun to read pages laced with practical tips.

Survival Kit $12.50

We asked ourselves what helpful items travelers have a hard time finding on their own and came up with the Back Door traveler's "Survival Kit." So, here they are, our 10 essentials, in one easy-to-carry package. It's new. It's useful. It'll save you a pile of headaches.

Eurail Passes
Send Eurail form with check for the pass and a proposed itinerary and list of questions. Receive within two weeks train pass and free cassette tape-recorded evaluation of trip plans by registered mail. Because of this unique service, Rick Steves sells more train passes than anyone in the Pacific Northwest.

RICK STEVES BUDGET TRAVEL SEMINARS are taught to groups and colleges throughout the West Coast. Write for info.

All orders include: rubber universal sink stopper and a one year's subscription to our quarterly Back Door Travel Newsletter. Sorry, no credit cards. Send checks to:

"EUROPE THROUGH THE BACK DOOR"

111 4th Ave. N.   Edmonds, WA 98020   tel. (206) 771-8303

Travel Guides from
John Muir Publications

I'd like to order the terrific travel guides checked below...

Quantity	Title	Each	Total
	Europe Through the Back Door—*Steves*	$11.95	
	Europe 101: History Art & Culture for Travelers—*Steves*	$9.95	
	Asia Through the Back Door—*Steves & Gottberg*	$11.95	
	Great Britain in 22 Days—*Steves*	$5.95	
	Spain & Portugal in 22 Days—*Steves*	$5.95	
	Complete Guide to Bed & Breakfasts, Inns & Guesthouses In the U.S. & Canada—*Lanier*	$12.95	
	Elegant Small Hotels—*Lanier*	$12.95	
	The People's Guide to Mexico (Revised)—*Franz*	$11.95	
	Mexico in 22 Days—*Rogers & Rosa*	$5.95	

Non-U.S. payments must be in U.S. funds drawn on a U.S. bank.	Subtotal	$
	Shipping	$1.75
METHOD OF PAYMENT (CHECK ONE) / **Total Enclosed**		$

METHOD OF PAYMENT (CHECK ONE)

☐ Charge to my (circle one): MasterCard VISA

☐ Check or Money Order Enclosed (Sorry, no CODs or Cash)

Credit Card Number

☐☐☐☐☐☐☐☐☐☐☐☐☐☐

Expiration Date ☐☐–☐☐

Signature x _____
Required for Credit Card Purchases

Telephone: Office (___) _____ Home (___) _____

Name _____

Address _____

City _____ State _____ Zip _____

Send to: John Muir Publications
P.O. Box 613
Santa Fe, NM 87504-0613
(505) 982-4078

Please allow 4-6 weeks for delivery.